Loose change

8 August '94

To Mum
with love & warm wishes

" Come Friday burn the
   factory to the ground...."
                    (p 50)

Ian x

First published in Great Britain in 1994 by *POETRY NOW*
1-2 Wainman Road, Woodston, Peterborough PE2 7BU

All Rights Reserved

Copyright Contributors 1994

Cover Design by Mark Rainey

Printed and bound in Great Britain by Forward Press, Peterborough

Loose change

Edited by
Ian Walton

ACKNOWLEDGEMENTS

The editor and publisher gratefully acknowledge permission to reproduce the following in this book:

Roger Woodis
Church Militant
Published *New Statesman and Society*

Simon Armitage
To Poverty After Laycock
First published in *Book of Matches*, Faber & Faber

Carol Ann Duffy
Mule
First published *The Guardian*

Foreword
From *Sir Thomas More*
Published *A Choice of Shakespeare's Verse*, Faber & Faber 1991

FOREWORD
Selected by Ted Hughes

Grant them remov'd, and grant that this your noise
Hath chid down all the majesty of England;
Imagine that you see the wretched strangers,
Their babies at their backs, with their poor luggage,
Plodding to th' ports and coasts for transportation,
And that you sit as kings in your desires,
Authority quite silenc'd by your brawl,
And you in ruff of your opinions clothed,
What had you got? I'll tell you. You had taught
How insolence and strong hand should prevail,
How order should be quell'd - and by this pattern
Not one of you should live an aged man;
For other ruffians, as their fancies wrought,
With selfsame hand, self reasons and self right
Would shark on you, and men like ravenous fishes
Would feed on one another.
You'll put down strangers,
Kill them, cut their throats, possess their houses,
And lead the majesty of law in liom
To slip him like a hound. Say now the king
(As he is clement, if th' offender mourn)
Should so much come too short of your great trespass
As but to banish you - whither would you go?
What country, by the nature of your error,
Should give you harbour? Go you to France or Flanders,
To any German prince, to Spain or Portugal,
Nay, anywhere that not adheres to England,
Why, you must needs be strangers. Would you be pleas'd
To find a nation of such barbarous temper
That, breaking out in hideous violence,
Would not afford you an abode on earth,
Whet their detested knives against your throats,
Spurn you like dogs, and like as if that God
Ow'd not nor made not you, nor that the elements
Were not all appropriate to your comforts,
But charter'd unto them - what would you think
To be thus us'd? This is the strangers' case,
And this your mountainish inhumanity.

From *Sir Thomas More*
William Shakespeare

INTRODUCTION
by Ian Walton

It could be argued that most poetry is retrospective and that poets can become mere observers to the ills of the word: reporters of events. Certainly one only has to look at the great 'War Poets' to see that if poetry changes anything it is certainly a long, slow process.

The pleasure in selecting the poems for inclusion in this book, for me, was a hope that 'this one could be different': the poets could have an immediate effect.

Possibly the last reason one writes a poem is for money (the pay is better at MacDonald's) but every contributor to Loose Change has in fact done this and I hope that this odd fund-raising method brings the money rolling in.

Yes, it would be good to raise a worthwhile sum for a worthwhile cause but it would also be a triumph for poetry; for all the poets included; and for the thousands of writers who sent their work to Poetry Now in an attempt to help 'War On Want'.

In the pages of this book you will find nationally recognised poets alongside the hitherto unknown. You will find the old and the young, but all the poems have a common thread: enough is enough, it is time for the world to change, and if all we have are words then let us put them into action.

CONTENTS

Title	Author	Page
Waiting in Macedonia	Brain Patten	1
Dives and Lazarus	John Heath-Stubbs	1
Mule	Carol Ann Duffy	2
Privilege	Graham Guest	2
Hungers	Evlynn Sharp	3
To Poverty	Simon Armitage	4
The Border Builder	Carol Rumens	5
Untitled	James Moodie	6
Evergreens	Dannie Abse	6
Always	U A Fanthorpe	7
Too Easy	Helen Taylor	8
Point On Bosnia?	John Jones	8
The Blood Bath	Katherine Griffey	9
What's In A Name?	Joey Pumford	10
An Extremely Important Academic	Frances Childs	10
The Maize-Folk Are Returning	Rhys Evans	11
My Forest	Rhiannon Jones	12
Shelving	David Jackson	12
Waiting	Trisha Ashley	13
Talk-Over Town	Gavin Ewart	14
Don't Believe It, Don"t Believe It . . .	Tommy	14
A Black Child In The News	Liz Saville	15
Church Militant	Roger Woddis	16
A Passing Glance	Jacqueline Ferreira	17
And I Feel Ashamed	Patrick McManus	17
Bombshell	Hamish Niven	18
Sleeping Gentle	Caroline Paice	19
Some Towns Have Fallen	Barbara Maskens	20
The Innocents	James Lennie	20
Amongst The Rubble Of The Baltic Exchange	Nick Galen	21
Beaten By The System	S R McCormick	22
Leftovers	Max Hafler	22
Hunger Eats The Seed	Hazel Archard	23

Soho Saturdays	Paul Campbell	24
House Guest	Toby Litt	24
News Child	C M O'Connell	25
Swansong (A Prayer For Freedom)	Kevin Cowdall	26
The General Rule	Markus Wagner	27
Lament To Christmas In Sarajevo	Jonathan Stephenson	28
No Angel Song	Helene McLeod	28
Man-Hate	Rachel Kendall	29
Andrew	Thomas H Green	30
Street Children	Nola Small	30
My Crushed Child	Murray Pannett	31
Skin	Henry Ward	32
Uncharged	Alan Theasby	33
The Poor	Bill Greenwell	34
The Balance	Nathan Loynes	35
Breakdown	Patricia Guerra	36
Tube Station	Michael C Miller	37
Human Degradation	David Conway	38
The Earth	Michael Burton	38
Peace	John Burns	39
Mogadishu	Victtoria Vaughan	40
No Thank You	Gillie Bolton	40
There Will Always Be An However	Hayley Darrington	41
Brother Wyn	Gareth Calway	42
For You	Bill Dancy	42
Poem For John	Merlin Evans	43
But Couldn't She?	Dee Scott	44
Voluntary Blindness	Kyriacos Moysi	44
The Totters	Geoff Fenwick	45
The Box	Jane MacNamee	46
Territories	Alan M Kent	46
Elephant Eternity	Adrian Mitchell	47
Place Of The Water: For All Those Who Together Make A Well	Marilyn Carter	48

Untitled	Lucy Williams	48
F Words	J P Portlock	49
Factory - Fragment From A Diary	Ian Duckett	50
Grudgements	Aidan Baker	50
Charity Begins At Home	Suman Ghosh	51
Finding His Feet	Don Patter	52
Haiku	Anthony Cox	52
Back In The Nineties	Mark A Goodwin	53
Rain	A K Whitehead	54
There Are Times	Richard Gallie	55
Gallows In My Eyes (An Apology For Apathy)	Stuart Elden	55
To Change My Mind	Don Reeve	56
Double Check	Mark Blackmore	56
October Woods	Michael Facherty	57
How Many Fallen Heroes?	Daniel Etherington	58
Mind	E A Mottershaw	59
Untitled	Jon Pyper	60
Human Rights Begin With Breakfast	Angie Gold	61
Strength	Nuzhat Jabinh	62
Skin Deep	Alison Hill	62
London Lady	Robert Galer	63
Simple Desperation	Pip G Fitzpatrick	63
Devastation	Elizabeth Grantham	64
Refugees	Pauline Kirk	64
Letter From The Nursing Home	Maeve Reid	65
Come My Great Patriot	Eric Nixon	66
United Nations' Building	Ron Woollard	66
Building Bridges	Cicely Herbert	67
Sorry Souls	Calum Miller	68
Sri Lanka - May 1992	Stephen Faulkner	68
Your Bill	Jacob Bush	69
Liberty Island - New York	John Dougherty	70
One Question	John Agard	70
Just A Spade	Judith P Powe	71

Title	Author	Page
Untitled	R D Murray	72
Crisis In Africa	D Carter	72
Wide Eyes	David Golledge	73
Metamorphosis	Solomon Blue-Waters	74
The Rover And The Blanket	Wendy Hill	74
Cuba Libre	Jean McNeil	75
Slow Death	Adrienne Lewis	76
18th Century : Re-Visited	Jon Hopper	76
Taboo	Eilish Martin	77
Dust Trail To Calvary	P G McCormack	78
Patience II	Julian Sharples	79
Treelessness	Emily Marbach	80
The Problem With The World Today	Marina Gaze	81
All Staff	David Topliff	82
Inheritance	Thomas Land	83
Me And You	David Whatley	83
I Am	Karen Jorgensen	84
The Children In Angola	Janet E Greenyer	84
Hate Poem	Sara Whitmarsh	85
Exiles	Jenny Vuglar	86
Lost	James O'Grady	86
Over Here	Adrian Spendlow	87
Fed Up!	Peter Shenlack	88
Destiny	Betty Elliott	88
Party Politics	Stephen Neal	89
New York, New York	Alan Manford	90
Untitled	Sue Dunn	90
In The Shit	D-Zine	90
The Photograph	V S Petheram	91
Not Have Not Have-Not	M Everingham	92
Civil War	William Young	92
1994	Carolyne Pike	93
Untitled	Sophie Pasarin	94
What A Place!	Jeffa Kay	94
Balance Sheet	Adrian Shaw	95
Untitled	Jeremy Ryan	96
Repercussions	John Hamilton	96

Title	Author	Page
Brief Encounter On A London Transport Platform	Eileen Simpson	97
The Last Child	D Leach	98
God's Blunder	Geoff Broady	98
Dress	Melanie Herring	99
Toys Of War	Jon Perigud	100
Inside Sadness	P Jilks	101
Untitled	Kathleen Wratten	102
Choice	Gwenyth Webb	102
The Pensioner And The Pot-Plant	Mary Cowan	103
The Right To Feel My Pain	Dave Miller	104
My Friends, Big Changes Are On The Way Soon	Hazel Lezah	104
In These Days	Michael Wixon	105
Two Lives	Fran Shortridge	106
Utopia?	Suzanne Kushner	106
There Is A Lesson In That	Maureen Scott	107
Homeless	Peter Whiteley	108
A Gulf Between	David Hill	108
Earth Apples (For Christopher Columbus)	Matthew Carter	109
Why Do They Show Only The Worst Face Of Our People	Bethan Hatherall	110
Blue Sky Over Bosnia	Emma Cable	110
Think	Saeed Farouky	111
The Fly	Andrew Nash	112
Late Night Watershed	James Mitchinson	112
Respect	V Greenfield	113
Shadows	Robin Mason	113
Womankind	Emma Jane Louise Buckley	114
War	David Leith	114
Love	Andrea Warunek	115
M40	Jason Oddy	115
Parallel Seasons	Marian Griffin	116
Dictatorship	Claire Barnes	116

Beloved People	Joan R Gilmour	117
Images	Russell Mills	118
Naaman	Jocelyn S Downey	118
Doesn't Matter	Lindsey-Jane Stewart	119
Prisoner Of Conscience	Irena Uderska	120
No-Man's Land	Fiona McCurdy	120
Nicaraguan Raincoat	Anne Murray	121
Untitled	Catherine Barton	122
Changes	Emma Shaw	122
The Sands	Nicholas Hayden	123
The Prison Boats	Zoé Teale	124
The Tree	Rebecca Holyhead	124
The Last Bus Crowd	Jamie Spracklen	125
Message From The Mayor	Reg Mares	126
Operation	J G Paterson	126
Start Again	Wolfgang Küchler	126
A Teenager's Dream	Paula Thomas	127
Burger Bar (USA)	John Hatton Davidson	128
Poetic Justice	Ruth Johannsen	129
The Lament Of Brick Lane	Ralph J Lawrence Connor	130
Rights	Josephine Blyth	130
Among Girls In Wartime	Krystyna Lejk	131
The End Of The Century	Rodrigo Fino	131
History Will Teach Us Nothing	Claire Motler	132
Injustice In General	Darin Brown	132
TV Heaven	Stephen Thorne	133
Eleison	Ralph Hoyte	133
Sugarwire	Paul Tremlett	133
Untitled	Amanda Watkins	134
Untitled	Steel Rosehip	135
Unforgettable	Julie McDonald	135
Warmth	Christian Walker	135
Untitled	Annick Lauren McKenzie	136
Victims Of Reality	Binta Sultan	136
Three Children	Cliff James	137
Beyond The Streets	Angus Landman	138
Disregarded	Kate Everington	138
The Way	Ann Wallis	139

Title	Author	Page
Marching To The Same Tune	Sean McMahon	140
Fiend	Zehria Ibrahimi	140
Christmas - Black And White - 1993	Jane Nyman	141
The Way To Stop	Ruth Faulkner	142
Search For Credence And Sanctuary	Gordon Gellatly	142
War 1 - 2 - ?	Adam Kisch	143
A Little Rye	John Conolly	144
The Homeless	Chris Mandell	144
Blessed Are The Merciful	Stella Gilder	144
Pictures From Africa	Jaquetta Benjamin	145
Ethnic Minority	Kirsten Pollard	146
Life Line	Jennifer Tucket	146
Work Hard	Steve Verrall	147
The Dagger	Paul Sharkey	148
Our Third World	Patricia Hynes	148
Goodbye Century	Gemma Reynolds	149
On Feeling A Coming Of A Chill	Andry Anastasiou	150
Question	Gareth Cavill	151
Words	D Kennedy	151
My Favourite War	Mostafa Woola	152
The Yellow Sky	Helen Dunmore	153
Bard At The Bar! (We Get Requests)	Paul Nicklin	154
One Question From A Bullet	John Agard	155
The Hero At The End Of The Century	Eamonn O'Neill	155
The Third Side	Lea Farmer	156
Sarajevo	Christopher Straker	157
Death	Jamie Muir	157
Dropping Pennies	Hammy	158
Cardboard Avenue	Olawale Akinlade	159
The Day Before	Julia Black	160
In The Cold	Milly Rumba	160
The Greedy West	Anne Wade	161
One Night's Victory	Dirkwood Marley Wad	162

WAITING IN MACEDONIA

In an empty hotel on the border
Of a country with no army,
The rooms shuttered, the pool
Given over to mosquitoes,
The Coca-Cola signs and travel adverts,
Kitch exhibits from a museum now.
In the middle-class suburbs
Children play with useless bank-notes,
Furtive adults hoard petrol,
In upstairs rooms anxious suitcases,
Pre-packed, await the starter's gun.
The sudden realisation: the dispossessed
Are not necessarily the poor.
Down in the town the sidewalk cafes
Bubble with rumours. Like clothes
That have been locked away too long,
Old prejudices are aired. Someone
Mentions the British. Someone
Mentions the Greeks. Someone
Mentions the Albanians. Someone
Admits they don't understand.
Someone orders a coffee and a doughnut,
And whistles after a pretty girl who is passing.

Brian Patten

DIVES AND LAZARUS

Dives fared sumptuously every day
On free-range eggs and organically grown vegetables;
Lazarus lay at Dives' gate,
And the dogs would lick his sores.
Dives regularly subscribed
To a fund for rehousing the dogs
In a centrally heated, air conditioned kennel complex.

John Heath-Stubbs

MULE

And when I got to eat, what I got to eat
was 80 condoms, packed, a bowl of oats.

20 days swallow, swallowing each one neat.
Red gravy bubbled up from my raw throat.

Then pills to clog the hole. A midnight boat.
Then a London plane, the window seat.

All this for cash. The contact I must meet
they said would know me by my yellow coat.

All wrong. Inside my gut, a seeping, queasy heat.
Then nothing. Darkness. When I could, I wrote

Your mother loves you with her life. One note.
May Queen of England pardon this poor cheat.

Carol Ann Duffy

PRIVILEGE

He read once when he was small
That at meals where you are given
More than one set of knives and forks
You should start from the outer ones
And work your way in
And that different drinks
Go in different glasses

It must be sad he thought
To live in what they call
The Third World
And not be able to read
You could easily embarrass yourself at dinner

Graham Guest

HUNGERS

How can folk say there's not the animal in us?

Why, look at that solitary old man who crawled
on Somalia, broadcast by satellite for breakfast
TV. Sitting rooms flood with him. Shaken skeleton,
his back horizontal, palms struggling to rake land,
find grain. Stretched above small insects.
His jawbone probing the dust.

A reporter said three million were starving,
and there were looters with different hunger.
But looming behind the summary piece,
it's the skelf of a man who draws my attention,
his old roped body unremarked. For not one
man or woman ran to help the elderly man then,
although the slot lasted for maybe three minutes
(which is long for a morning news byte).

Instead, the sound recordist concentrated
on the sweaty journalist.
The camera operator focused on getting
the daylight just right.
The story was turned into a perfect mirror
for drowsy tea-swillers.

I was dumbfounded how no-one went immediately
to lift up the old man in their stronger arms, hold him
steady, explaining, 'This is how I love you, man,'
and enquire about his name, his lifetime.

No, the man is composed on TV like an old lion
with a soundless roar being drummed into him.

Evlynn Sharp

TO POVERTY
after Laycock

You are near again, and have been there
or thereabouts for years. Pull up a chair.
I'd know that shadow anywhere, that silhouette
without a face, that shape. Well, be my guest.
We'll live like sidekicks - hip to hip,
like Siamese twins, joined at the pocket.

I've tried too long to see the back of you.
Last winter when you came down with the flu
I should have split, cut loose, but
let you pass the buck, the bug. Bad blood.
It's cold again; come closer to the fire, the light,
and let me make you out.

How have you hurt me, let me count the ways:
the months of Sundays
when you left me in the damp, the dark,
the red, or down and out, or out of work.
The weeks on end of bread without butter,
bed without supper.

That time I fell through Schofield's shed
and broke both legs,
and Schofield couldn't spare to split
one stick of furniture to make a splint.
Thirteen weeks I sat there till they set.
What can the poor do but wait? And wait.

How come you're stuck with me? Go see the Queen,
lean on the doctor or the dean,
breathe on the major,
squeeze the mason or the manager,
go down to London, find a novelist at least
to bother with, to bleed, to leech.

On second thoughts, stay put.
A person needs to get a person close enough
to stab him in the back.
Robert Frost said that. Besides,
I'd rather keep you in the corner of my eye
than wait for you to join me side by side
at every turn, on every street, in every town.
Sit down, I said sit down.

Simon Armitage

THE BORDER BUILDER

No sooner had one come down,
   Than he began building again:
My bricks, O my genuine bricks
   Made of my genuine blood!
O who would we be without borders?
   'So which one are you?' he said
And stuck out his hand to me.
   Birth certificate? Passport?
Which side are you on? Which side?
   Merrily he unrolled
Starry dendrons of wire
   To give his wall ears and eyes.
'Qualifications?' he said.
   Residence permit? Tattoo?
Which colour are you? Which colour?
   'No colour,' he said, 'no good.'
He took my only passport.
   He slammed it down on the wire.
My hand, O my genuine hand!
   'This is a border,' he said.
A border likes blood. Which side
   Is your bloody hand on, which side?

Carol Rumens

UNTITLED

Sun bleeds,
Over a horizon that is fast closing in.
October shadows,
Creep across a freeze-dried landscape.
And every last traitor bird,
Has stopped singing.
This is the way the world ends,
Without even a whimper.

James Moodie

EVERGREENS

I

'Death? That's for other people,'
Billy Lucas used to say,
sad, sunny-side up, verbal Billy Lucas.

It's winter now in his closed shop-doorway.

He used to roll up his trousers,
dart towards an autumn tree
quicker than a dog-hunted cat
and, at the quivering top, shout out
with spotless joy, 'I am immortal!'

Sometimes he seemed to be
the happiest patient
in that hospital of sorrows.

It's winter now in the grounds of St. Ebbas.

The tall deciduous trees have staged
their own phoney funerals
(such morbid, such colourful rehearsals)
and pose for black and white photography.

Who'll cry, 'Long live manic denial,'
esteem the cedar and the yew
and all euphoric Evergreens?

II
It's summer now in the Municipal Gardens.
I know a consoling fountain there. Ssh, surprise:
a cherub, copper greenish-blue, juggles
four open-mouthed, water-spouting fish. Look! One more
peeing trout has landed between his thighs.

I pass a hoarse-voiced, overbearded crazy
on a wooden bench. It seems that he prays
to this small fat idol who juggles behind
sunlit shatterings of water. The cherub, of course,
smiles on - insouciant and ecstatic and blind.

Dannie Abse

ALWAYS

There was always a beast,
And always a human to take it on:
Someone from Samaria; a lamp-in-hand lady;
A body with a cooking-pot, and a pinch of goodwill.

But in our day the beast is bolder,
Thrusts his tainted head into our snug
Domestic screens, shows us the bones,
The shrouds, the fly-filled eyes.

We aren't Samaritans; we have no lamps;
Even a cooking-pot is hard to find.
Our bag of tricks: the versatile goodwill
Of pay-by-plastic, cheque, fax, giro, Switch.

There is always a beast,
And always a human to take it on,
A generous heart to say
I saved this for my tomorrow,

But you need it for your today.

U A Fanthorpe

TOO EASY

Once,
I wrote a poem,
On a paper bag,
About someone I knew
Who died.
Each time I read it
It hurt.
Pulled my guts
inside out.
Made me remember
What it's really like
to care.
Then.
I lost it.

Helen Taylor

POINT ON BOSNIA?

These women
grouped informally
not posing
too shocked
to be shocked
by the flash
and click of cameras

are blown
to black and white
to positions
above the bold
barbed words
that say

'The men who raped them
 were just normal men
 what does that tell us
 about normal men.'

normal men like me?

too shocked
to be shocked
by the flash
and click.

John Jones

THE BLOOD BATH

It is hard to think about war when I'm warm and drinking tea.
It is often inconvenient for me to interrupt my life
and think about death.
I have large problems of my own, how to afford the things that I own
how to manage, this month, the car and the phone,
my lovers, my parents, my pets,
I'm vexed as to how I'm supposed to fit anything else in
and then all this about death!

I wish it would just leave me alone.

But then another bloody child dies with large eyes
and I go all soppy and cry sometimes
when I'm in the mood.
The best cure I find for all this misery is to run a nice hot bath
and soak for a long time.
I find this very soothing and it takes my mind off the blood issue,
the waste of tissue and I forget all the stuff on the telly,
the stink, the torture, the bloated bellies,
I find all my worries disappear.

I would like to help, but not at the moment
the war has called at the wrong time.
Don't you just find it?
When you're in the bath the phone always fucking rings.

Katherine Griffey

WHAT'S IN A NAME?

So, you changed your name
from Ceaser to Pope.
From Czar to Chairman.
Then, with your redcross
and your red flag.
You set out to change the world.
You have new names now.
Freedom and democracy
Law and order.
And still you kill!

Joey Pumford

AN EXTREMELY IMPORTANT ACADEMIC

'Excuse me please
I've just finished a very
important
report, which proves beyond
doubt
that if you're unemployed
you're poor.
My massive enquiries
took years to complete
and actually funding was a
bit of a bugger
but we managed to raise
the required amount
And now I'd like to see
How the cabinet ministers
wriggle out of this one
Ha!
I say, Bernard, pass
the claret
please.'

Frances Childs

THE MAIZE-FOLK ARE RETURNING

In the early eighties, persecuted and brutalised by the Guatemalan army, some 100,000 peasant farmers from northern Guatemala sought refuge in southern Mexico. In January 1993 the first block of 2600 returned to a country not much changed since they left 1300 years ago. On December 9th 1993, another 1300 arrived in Quiché. Now more and more are planning to return. 'Los hombres de maiz retornan a su país.'

The nightmare dusts have settled
Yet even now a passing breeze can raise
Distorted forms

The maize-folk are returning

In ancient lands
Roots of dark vines grip
Husks of the tortured dead
Though from the shade
Shine shy smiles

The maize-folk are returning

Tightly clenched clusters
Of souls blank
From the thud of shells
The rhythmic stutter of steel

But slowly watered, stirring
Again into flower, turning
Again in the ancient round of the sun
Which in its eye enfolds
Those past
And those that are yet to be
The old clasped in a new future

The maize-folk are returning

Rhys Evans

MY FOREST

My land has gone;
My hope has flown away;
My canopy of green has vanished;
My river is dried up.

I hear their harsh voices,
'Cut them down,
It's only a few acres,
It won't hurt a fly.'

When morning awoke
I used to hear the screech of monkeys,
And the carefree whistling of the birds.
But no more.
All I can hear now
Is the crashing of hardwood giants
By the one armed monsters.

Dawn fell over the forest
Like a sheet of pure white silk.
But the forest does not seem
To be its lively self today.

Gorillas stare with sad, tearful eyes,
All the trees are gone,
And mother nature grieves.

Rhiannon Jones

SHELVING

I see the rubber feet on the shelves -
among the books about the Third World
I have to remind myself
these are small feet -
artificial limbs for children
I'm so used to artificial thinking
it is an effort to feel

I'm putting up shelves at home -
trying to go back to art after several years
dead years
not feeling
politics or art?
I've tried to want neither
escape both

The rubber is brown -
hardly Michelangelo
but does that matter to the Asian child?
So they don't play football for their country
no great loss
but the sex cuts deep -
will they be able to find wives and husbands
have complete homes where shelves
store the memories of feeling?

David Jackson

WAITING

With the morning sun come ashes,
in showers,
like petals from a shaken tree.
And people as ever run screaming
from the light,
to burn their eyes
with endless watching of each other.
Waiting,
in the far places,
for death's tomorrow.
And rivers run
backwards with bodies;
And birds have fled.

Trisha Ashley

TALK-OVER TOWN

You despise them at your peril -
Charming Charlie, Cheerful Cheryl -
they sing *profits up!* But what comes down
misses the poor in Take-over Town!

Charlie's mum is a Prime Minister,
so his inside track is sinister -
Clive James thinks Cheryl wears the crown,
she's the sexiest thing in Take-over Town!

If you can wine a wog and charm him
he'll be pleased to let you arm him!
A bit of bribery, a bit of brown,
it's easy stuff in Take-over Town!

Knock off orchestra, art and gallery,
put half a million on his salary!
In that circus he's no clown -
he's the likely lad in Take-over Town!
Victories: Blenheim, Malplaquet, Ramillies!
The war against one-parent families!
A thousand-quinea evening gown
is much admired in Take-over Town!

Is God happy? Despised? Neglected?
No *Peace on Earth* - so long expected -
and the poor poorer. It gets you down,
when you think about Take-over Town!

Gavin Ewart

DON'T BELIEVE IT, DON'T BELIEVE IT . . .

It did not happen then:
six million people did not die.
Babies were not speared
on bayonets.
It's lies, all lies.

    High on a mountainside
    an old man weeps.

It did not happen then:
there were no killing fields; no rape,
no-one was feared.
There were no crimes.

    High on a mountainside
    an old man weeps.

It did not happen then;
it could not happen now:
how could we turn our backs
so many times?

    High on a mountainside
    the old man weeps.

You ask me why
my poems do not rhyme.

Tommy

A BLACK CHILD IN THE NEWS

We love the skeleton child's
spaniel eyes -
her last few hours make prime time.

Here's today's hot property,
until the paper-buying public surfeit
on the wasted limbs
and the camera turns to
new monstrosities.
She's had her fifteen minutes.

And what was she to me?
A morsel for consumption
between soaps and advertisements.

Liz Saville

CHURCH MILITANT
The church of England's report on the government's inner city policy has been described by an unnamed Cabinet Minister as 'pure Marxist theology'

The church's single function
Is to relieve an itch:
She pours on holy unction
To sanctify the rich.
Beyond suburban borders
Lie acres of despair,
Above the lower orders
The upper class at prayer.

Behold the inner city,
A temple to Our Lord,
Where there is talk of pity
And cash we can't afford.
One holy theme inspires them
Who serve their Master's will:
The simple faith that fires them
Are weapons that can kill.

Bow down before your Maker,
Before your betters kneel,
Give ear to Kenneth Baker
And follow at his heel.
Reject the Marxist clients
Who do the church such hurt;
Believe in *self-reliance*,
And vomit down your shirt.

Roger Woddis

A PASSING GLANCE

I walked straight past you, thinking
Nothing in particular.
Just another obstruction on the street,
To step over.
And then you looked at me, sinking
Livid eyes like knives,
That told me too much for one brief,
Passing glance.
They asked for something that
The shallow clatter
Of my coins dropped in your hat,
Surely did not give.

Jacqueline Ferreira

AND I FEEL ASHAMED

And the dear sweet dear
dear grey haired lady
at the resident's committee says
what about the homeless?
With their drink and dogs
spoiling the atmosphere
not what we want
not want we want at all
not in Raynes Park
they should go back
go back to Vauxhall
go back to Waterloo
and they all agree
and I feel sad
and I feel sick
and I feel ashamed.

Patrick McManus

BOMBSHELL

Garbled message:
'There's a bomb on Oxford Street.
It's going off in three minutes.'

Click and hum, line's dead.
Silent bombshell. Stomach and heart drop
Can you see the hate in the policeman's eyes?

What happens next?
He knows the fear
remembers the sound of death

Two minutes fifty and silence
Pin drops two hundred yards away
Afraid eyes search up and down

Eternity is ten seconds
Our Father
Who art in Heaven
Hallowed be Thy name . . .

Unseen unheard prayers

Son on father's shoulders
'Daddy, why can't we go into the shop?'

10.9 Two seconds gone

8.7   Generations born, live and die in peace.

6.5   Stars explode and planets evolve.

4.3   Four heartbeats a snuffle, the blue wall reeks fear

2.1   Eyes close. Prayers and moans to respective Gods.
      A Catholic cries, 'I'm so sorry.'

It's due, no birds no traffic
The silent bomb. The day stops and life waits

It comes.

Hamish Niven

SLEEPING GENTLE

My eyes are open wide;
hiding, wide eyes in the smoky mist of darkness,
rocking steadily, left and right.

Walls, walled in wallpaper,
tricked by walls of *special offers*;
falling asleep in cement.

Drowsy, tired eyes, won't relax so
images run like picture shows
across the lids.

The tape of memories rolls on:
I am sent away in silence
for the last time; I run away in fear.

Cold, under feather duvets.
Under hallowed, hollowed blankets, blue.
My skin burns with lament.

Lips are stamped with frost,
so I open out my hands;
not to the poor, but as the poor.

The unrelenting wind sends
chatters of shivers to talking teeth.
Do join in my conversation.

A foetal floating frame of mind
for I curl up; knees tucked
under my dirty chin.

Winter will never end:
Toes will transform in to icicles forever,
in my sleeping bag of soot.

The past is catching up,
though I am too weary to run.
This life will only take winners.

Caroline Paice

SOME TOWNS HAVE FALLEN

Some towns have fallen
into the hands of the invader -
some piles of stones, water supplies.

The possessions of ancient families
lie in ruin - because the invader
cares nothing for our tradition.

But the people keep a good heart
being of noble race.

Their blood resists this war
which for many years
has occupied the thoughts and strategies
of those in power.
Meanwhile we tend our fields, our olives,
planted before our grandfathers' remembrance,

should we burn our groves -

The enemy is here to stay, invaders everywhere
what is to become of us
we have not been told what to do
and would rather stay,
see our children live.

Barbara Maskens

THE INNOCENTS

'No thanks,' said the soldier,
As the little Belfast boy,
Shot him,
Once,
Through the head.

His mother would be proud.

James Lennie

AMONGST THE RUBBLE OF THE BALTIC EXCHANGE

East-enders fly around like wasps
west-enders fly around like drones
right-wing men fly around covering cracks as they appear
a pall of insecticide floats above the city
diluting in the breeze
mannequins' boils leak money in the windows of Liberty's
blue officials and shop assistants press weeping stigmata
dip their fingers in the ooze
they can't stop themselves
they turn a bluer shade of blue than they were already
while the ground on which they built their bungalows
subsides

over bowling-greens
statues of Thatcher lean
metal-fatigued
Elizabeth plods on symbolically not knowing what else to do
while her subjects fight over scraps of casual work
and flying the world like a carpet
Thatcher tells her story to anyone who'll buy it

are there any escalators to carry us out?
are there any elevators to lift us up?

the blitz is over but not completely
and we emerge amongst the rubble of the Baltic Exchange

aren't there any escalators to carry us up?
aren't there any escalators to carry us down?

we hope the bombing will end soon
though everyone knows there's little anyone can do
because what came before comes after
no matter what we do

Nick Galen

BEATEN BY THE SYSTEM

She was a single mum,
So you took away her benefits,
She was unemployed,
So you branded her *a scrounger.*
She went on the game,
        to pay for food for her child,
So you took her to court,
        and fined her.
She had no money to pay the fine,
So you locked her up in a cell.
She couldn't look after her child,
So you put him in care.
She couldn't bear to live that way,
So she hung herself in her cell.

System - One   Innocent victim - Nil

S R McCormick

LEFTOVERS

Scrape
The scraps
Into the bin.

My mum says
'Faddy!
Some little lad
In Africa'd
Be glad of that!'

Stare
At the slops.
A gravywet nest
Of greens
For a curled worm
Of pigfat.

Think.
'Is there anyone
On earth
That hungry?'

Consumed
With guilt,
I spoon
The slops
Into an envelope
Addressed
'A CHILD IN AFRICA.'

I run
To my mum,
Beg her
Not to miss
The post.

The envelope
Bleeds gravy
On my palm.

Max Hafler

HUNGER EATS THE SEED

He never learnt to count or write or read,
But calculate he can
His likely living-span
From knowledge born of unremitting need,
By rote of endless toil
In long-eroded soil
Where seasons fail and hunger eats the seed.
This quickening of breath
Will soon be put to death:
Small starving scion of a dying breed.

Hazel Archard

SOHO SATURDAYS

Street dusters play
Midnight buskers
To Charlie's on the bottle
In the street
People meet, shake a smile
Wander by
Burger brothels beat time.
To salty fingers.
Frost bite lingers in the shadows
Dark with time
Jazz clubbers mingle
With street light singles
Little bra-ed, shady ladies
Recline on passenger seat trains
To fame and fortune
Up suicide alleys
With DPPs
On probation.

Paul Campbell

HOUSE GUEST

Death dropped round the other evening.
  Said he couldn't stay for long.
Stayed for supper, stayed for coffee,
  still I couldn't get him gone.

Death slept over till the morning.
  Missed the last bus home, he said.
In the morning, after breakfast,
  Death yawned and went back to bed.

How time flew till it was lunchtime!
  Death was caught up in a book.
There was nothing in the kitchen.
  'Don't worry,' said Death, 'I'll cook.'

Death has now been here a fortnight.
   Shows no sign of leaving yet.
Always mean to put it to him.
   Somehow, always, I forget.

Toby Litt

NEWS CHILD

Child of war
        flickering across my mind,
You have no nation, no colour, no home.
        Empty eyes, tangled limbs
            lie amongst destruction;
        Lit by unyielding albic flashes - intruding
            helpless on your pain.
Crimson tears of life
        track from your wretched body
Moonscarr'd by famine's caustic whip.

We stand apart
        afraid to offer comfort,
Reluctant to remember - or forget
          lest you infect us with a violent spore
        Causing our men to die
           Our children starve

            Absolved by aid!

Could we be bold
        give you family,
Bind ourselves your wounds
        share ourselves bread?
            Hope would be Peace

Your rebirth a Child of love!

C M O'Connell

SWANSONG (A PRAYER FOR FREEDOM)

Pity the free man,
for he has not the courage of his conviction -
To stand up and shout
'No! It shall not be!'

I fear not to defend that right,
have no dread of repression -
For, though you subdue the body,
the spirit cannot be suppressed.

You cannot hang faith
by the neck until it is dead.

You cannot stand conviction
against a wall and shoot it down.

You cannot exile principle
to a barren wasteland.

You cannot torture hope
into servile submission.

Though you keep me
in your deepest, darkest, most solitary cell,
a spark of light will filter through;
the belief will linger on.

For am I not the chalice
in which the sacred body is reborn?
While I exist, so shall
thy host be ever upraised.

And who is to say
that swans do not indeed
sing before they die?

Kevin Cowdall

THE GENERAL RULE

They set up the general rule
to keep the peace -
sold us fighter-planes,
we needed wheat,
built new capitals and
dams to hold up their investment,
we forced democracy and now the people pay.

They check our social progress,
say we're spending too much:
'Why should people help themselves?
They have to meet the payments.'

Maintain their right to profit
free the slave to better exploit,
we get loud, they put us down,
try revolution, nationalise,
go socialist? -
We get the fist.

Encouraged to compete,
we raise more beef to feed your dogs,
keep the starving off the plantation
so there's coffee on your table,
set-up factories with no controls . . .
you need wood? - We'll cut the forest down.

You say there is so much of what we sell
that what we sell is cheap,
but you make sure that everything
we need is out of reach.

Beat them at their own game -
grow cocaine?

Markus Wagner

LAMENT TO CHRISTMAS IN SARAJEVO

Pale, staring faces, disbelieving
Of the destruction brought
By those seeking *freedom, independence,*
Power.
The best-laid schemes of the *peacemakers*
Lie bleeding in the charred remains
Of the houses. The houses which once,
Filled with joy at the coming of the new year,
Rejoiced. Crushed.
By the mailed fist of *ethnic cleansing.*
Hope? Blue berets?
Impotent to end the suffering
In every household, every sheet.
The houses of God merely shelters
From the horror of human conflict
Peace? Goodwill toward men?
Tidings of joy? Crushed.
By the tanks and terrorists . . .

. . . Pale, staring face, lying
Dead on the street. The victim
A casualty of hatred
Between former brothers -
The scars of battle forever inscribed
Upon the weary heart of a forgotten race.

Jonathan Stephenson

NO ANGEL SONG

Those shepherds long ago
heard angels sing -
or so I'm told -
sense-tingling, mind-blowing
songs from outer space
filling the inner ear.

I strain my senses
but detect no sound,
save that of shrivelled infants
sucking at empty breasts;
I see no blinding visions,
only children blank-eyed
from mindless horrors.

O angels, sing again, for me,
flood my night sky with your light.
My heart is raw with grief
for young men aged by pain,
girls twisted by abuse,
numbed by neglect.
Tear-blinded I go astray
and stumble in the dark.

No visions then? No angels?
Only an olive grove and bloody sweat,
a cry of deep despair,
only a cross - but empty.

Lord help me where faith falters,
vision fades
and angels never sing.

Helene McLeod

MAN-HATE

Hit me, hit me and hit me again,
I ask for more because it's all I can take.
It's been going on for so long.
How do I cope, you ask.
Ha! I laugh in your faces,
I cope alright.
You see, it's all my fault,
That's what he tells me,
It's all my fault.

Rachel Kendall

ANDREW

Andrew is in blue jeans
    and has a yellow jacket.
Andrew's round at my house
    listening to the racket.
Andrew stands amid the space
    where speaker sound is best.
He bites his hand, then grinds his teeth,
    emitting hooting, ape-like sounds
    every now and then.
Transfers his weight from foot to foot,
    rapidly and jiggling;
    hunches neck and twists it down
    between his shoulder-blades.
    And squints
        and jerks
            and twitches.
Picks up objects from the shelf
    and smells them, rubs them on his face.
No genie appearing through
    and Andrew will return
    to the *special* home
    they call *Grassybanks*.
'One sandwich short,' - they say that too
    but bless his schizoid soul
        he loves the bass.
Thomas H Green

STREET CHILDREN

Warm water laps my feet
Where children sleep in shop corners.

Cactus shelters the lizards
Where children sleep in shop corners.

Bathing beauties bask under thatched huts
Where children sleep in shop corners.

Men sip suds at the bar
Where children sleep in shop corners.

Paragliders glide and tilt the sea
Where children sleep in shop corners.

Windsurfers wheel and spin
Where children sleep in shop corners.

Pelicans fill their beaks for a week
Where children sleep in shop corners.

Nola Small

MY CRUSHED CHILD

My love,
I want to be near to you,
to dance in your shadow,
be your support
in times of darkness.
Reach out your fingers -
let's join, create a union of spirits,
so much energy drains away,
taken by our world -
lost forever.
I wish to give to you,
to recharge you,
to restore
your dynamo;
which is being drained.
Your light is growing dim.
I will give you new life,
my love.
Hang on I will be there
in an instant;
but an instant
was too late.

Murray Pannett

SKIN

This skin, a witness to my scars
Of surgeon's scalpel, sliced, split
On stone grazed,
Picked, squeezed and scratched.
Beneath coarse cloth; bruised and punctured.

But witness also my intimacy:
Caressed and stroked
Of soft lips kissed
And soothing touch, skin on skin,
The sweaty balm of sex
Inducing pores of liquid breath
To wash my surface and embrace
The shell
That binds my body to myself.

That which we judge
And are by others judged
We call a shallow crust
But if hung high;
Skinned hares on hooks
The butcher's ware,
Glistening red muscle and bloody bone
We would not recognise.

For this skin is all
Our history
Tattooed deep and furrows scribed
The surface pocked
And marked with time
Unique and individual text;
Skin.

Henry Ward

UNCHARGED

Their pleasure malicious
in it trying
to degrade humiliate him but
he switched himself
off from years of practice bashed
against a wall and blocking out Mam's
black eyed tears their
convenient victim target took him in
their car they
had the power
to do
it
No one
will come if
you shout
for help they said Bend over fingers
up his bum gratuitous fullbody
search they called
it because they could it was
part of the game they had
the power their right
and left
him hours alone wondering
would they do if then at
last they let him
go and when he got
home shaky
then
he painted out his
anger

Alan Theasby

THE POOR

The poor are always without us,
The poor are always without:
We feel them within as if burrs on our skin,
Like dust in the eye, or stubble on chin,
And offer our benefit, doubt.

The poor are really beyond us,
The poor are really beyond:
We see them eat rusk when the day becomes dusk,
And each one a shadow, a phantom, a husk,
Till sleep makes our conscience abscond.

The poor are often before us,
The poor are often before:
We heard of their caste in the age before last
And pretend that their present is part of our past,
Like a wound we remember was raw.

The poor do not come across us,
The poor do not come across:
They hide in the chink of the light, in a blink,
In oblivion's well, and in memory's sink,
As silent, as quiet as moss.

The poor are existing about us,
The poor are existing, about:
And unless we regain a sense of their pain,
We'll be left with the helpless and hopeless refrain:
The poor are always without,
The poor are always without us,
The poor are always without.

Bill Greenwell

THE BALANCE

Please . . . I'm not a prophet, I'm a man with a license,
not to kill . . . But common-sense is not violence;
Defence. I uplift and shoot the gift,
avoid the lifetime bid, it's times like this
I'd like to . . . Pull a gun, on a pig,
but, inna UK. There's no NWA. Dig? . . . It.
I dug it, pick up a microphone and plug it, in.
I rap . . . I can't sing.
I try and think with my mind, not my *dingaling,*
that's why I don't grip my dick,
but, I stick my views down ya throat till it makes you sick.
It might be that my rhymes are too heavy,
but I go on an' on like an Ever Ready
battery. Some people laugh at me,
'cos kaleidoscopic my optic on humanity.
Psychotic: I lost my grip on reality.
Big deal! I build my own world in my brain,
Because I'll never live in yours. It's too insane.
An' if I try, I might die, an' I refuse to be a product
of an environment that man was never meant
to control, to the extent he does;
His grip in a bit will be a handful of dust.
An' still the sun beats down. An' I'm not brown,
I contradict I'm down with I'm the son of the devil.
I pick up the balance and put my mind on the level:
The sun gets hot, I not got UV ray protection,
'cos my father's father feared a black man's erection.
Either take my advice; think about things twice,
or stand on one pan of the balance . . . An' pay the price.

Nathan Loynes

BREAKDOWN

Like many other days
    I woke up and turned the radio on
    hoping to hear . . . hoping,
    though something deep inside me
    as always turned me off

Like many mornings
    and some other evenings
    the news was not so new:
    Bosnia, Africa, murderers, unemployment,
    and the lot

    and once more that aching pain
    was calling out
    something inside me,
    as always hurt a lot

Lacking understanding of my sorrow,
    I tried to alleviate their own
    pleading, asking, 'What about tomorrow?'
    'Don't worry,'
    That's all that I was told.
    The First World War, yes
    will heal them all
    (by now you should this know!)
    though first
    the prey will have to prove
    no less, to show
    they're really abandoned

Like many other days
    at no special turning,
    confused and lonely
    and badly wounded,
    I was the news -

I had to see the starving child
inside, within,
my one and only,
disguised by the spell
of the First World War,
neglected even worse
than those children abroad.

Patricia Guerra

TUBE STATION

I sit alone,
Hunched in silence.
Engulfed in a timeless,
Emotionless,
Void.

Thoughts drifting,
Meandering,
Slowly, slowly,
Dying . . .

A train explodes
From the tunnel.
I am defined.
Another crisis,
Crystallised at Christmas.
An image captured
in a rush of glass and steel.

It passes.
I dissipate, a cloud again.
I float above your heads,
Unseen in silence.

I am a scream in space,
A gasp in a vacuum.

Michael C Miller

HUMAN DEGRADATION

I
 stand
  and
   view
    a
     world,
      where
       my
        eyes
         can
          only
           see
            so
             far,
              then
               I
                shield
                 my
                  eyes
                   from
                    the
                     world,
                      because
                       my
                        heart
                         sees
                          more.

David Conway

THE EARTH

God stretched on a tree sees
Earth and her shores;
knows each sphere suffer its spreading foe;
feels each foe clog with dust, with pain . . .

God stretched on a tree sees a grey-bearded land,
where a vial has been poured. By a dying hand
Death's vortex was stirred;
And the winds were not washed
of their sorrow or sin.
God stretched on a tree
                            feels
their cry . . .
      grow dumb.

God stretched on a tree sees
a shining land
of barefoot children. But another dark hand
pours the violent poison which withers the mind.
And the note of the bellbird is choked in the throat.

God stretched on a tree knows the silence of death
And the void without tears

And will wrestle with both
On the Cross of the World
While the wounds
Are not numb.

Michael Burton

PEACE

Peace will never come to this world.
One certainty is it cannot,
because of egocentric, selfish man
and power lust, his harlot.
The only possible peace will be
inside each salvaged heart brought
back from the dungeon of complacency
where Faith and Hope and Love rot.

John Burns

MOGADISHU

It is easy to get the packages this far,
To the harbour, where waves lift spirits ashore,
But in the city, sterility rules by the gun,
Not government, the only sign of life lies
In the air; the decay of thirty thousand
Killed or wounded; seen also in the face
Of each soldier, insomniac, drugged hypnotist
Whose mood swings like a pendulum
May or may not gauge the correct passing era,
May or may not let you pass;
Trembling hands wrapped around a rocket launcher
Are aimed at you; that's freedom? Freedom a gun
Throttled hunger; hunger of mouth and convoy
Flying the flag of peace, of charity giving out
Hope of getting their engrained message across;
As the bomb or rifle terrorises, all powerful
Dictators scorch deserts, turn back times
And with them all white packages close
To decay, an end to a short life-span
A day or so away; by then there's nothing
But a few more holes dug to dispose
Of the unethical contents, other packages
Wrapped in calico accumulating as flies, and things
Carrying on as ever, simply a little harder to breathe.

Victtoria Vaughan

NO THANK YOU

She didn't feel so cold
when she was plump
and old men used to pinch her cheek;
all workmen always whistled at her,
and everyone said how happy she must be
having such eyes,
hair, thighs, breasts . . .

No-one loves her still.
But at least they look the other way
now her teeth are too big,
and her blue skin
a corset
over cheekbones.

She doesn't love her either:
so stuffed full,
gorged on self
she wants to spit her out;
always - that sick taste
of self.

Gillie Bolton

THERE WILL ALWAYS BE AN HOWEVER

Edging nearer to it,
now you're not in credit.
You owe them everything,
but have nothing
except yourself to give.

You say,
you need that rope to pull you in,
you need that rope to hang you from.
You'd rather face this bitter fate
than let it all drag on.

There is a choice,
however.
You can break through,
however.
Walk towards the light to see
there is a however,
(there will always be an however).

Hayley Darrington

BROTHER WYN

The old Stalinist makes his stand
Each end of his Saturday shift,
*Morning Star*s steady in his hand.
Like a poet among philistines,
Like a thief in the night;
Loved by a legion and with hardly a comrade,
Thirty-nine years in the wilderness;
Stands at the top of the market-day steps,
Life and soul of the Party.

'A lot of Labourism in this valley,
Son, not much socialism,'
He patiently argues and always wins
And never wins. Serves the community
On every committee, on every issue;
Stands as defeated Soviet yearly;
Is deserted by family, by union blocked.
'Why not do all the good you do
Under Labour's flag for the love of God?'

But his vision's a world without classes.
A worker asks, 'Why should I give
So chocos can sit on their arses?'
No academic questions here; nor
Cloistered-professor's distinctions:
He gives the line on colonial theft
And the Third World debt, simple as truth.
Then, at last, turns Labour councillor,
Is missed. In his place, workless youth.

Gareth Calway

FOR YOU

Because barbed wire scars the sun's light
and you won't be home tomorrow, either,
I will continue beneath the night.

I have learned and taught freedom as a right,
that the harvest is full and for all to gather,
because barbed wire scars the sun's light.

Because we live by spirit and not by might,
yet naked men dance in epileptic terror
I will continue beneath the night.

Where the shading of stone dulls faces from sight
hearts will weave threads as if for a lover,
because barbed wire scars the sun's light.

When love must swing beneath depth and height
to shake roots, take dreams to shatter,
I will continue beneath the night.

And should you lose yourself during the night,
to break, where earth thirsts and hungers
because barbed wire scars the sun's light,
I will continue beneath the night.

Bill Dancy

POEM FOR JOHN

Life's wounding; felt in bad blood,
Born brother for each other.
Green downs, linnet and lark summer skies,
Clear brooks, woods, holy to a child's eyes,
Drowned in a feud's flood.
Born brother to each other.
Muddy waters, deserts, slights,
Long visited in sleepless winter nights,
Scars unhealed. Are we ever brother,
Born brother to love each other?
Would language the hurt could balm,
Wait we only for death's alarm?

Merlin Evans

BUT COULDN'T SHE?

'Surely *something* can be done for her.
Help's available *everywhere* these days - not like it was.'
'Aye, and even then we never begged,'

'Actually I *would* like to give - but once you start . . .'
'Exactly! Where does it all end?
I work hard for me brass - give it to the likes of her? No fear!'

'She's feckless. Just sheer laziness. Just look at that disgusting old coat. Revolting.
If you ask me, it's all an act.'
'Yeah, like them gippos - riding around in fancy cars conned from suckers like us!'

'Get a job you slut! If I have to work like a dog, why shouldn't you?'

'Okay, fifty pence should do. Any more'd go on booze.'
'Well, she'll be alright. Won't she?'

Dee Scott

VOLUNTARY BLINDNESS

Cold and hungry and lost in thought,
Her sad eyes show the battle she has fought.
Soft cries for help fall on deaf ears,
As her will to live slowly disappears.
No-one can see her sitting in the street,
Even though she is there in amongst their feet.
Thinking, 'How can she survive? How can she cope?'
Without warmth, care, comfort and hope.
You make your way home trying to forget,
Pretending everything's fine, pushing out the regret.
But she'll still be there, haunting your mind,
Until you wake up and stop being blind.

Kyriacos Moysi

THE TOTTERS

The seagulls
over Bidston Tip
scrounge for the scraps
which the bin lorries
bring, below them
forty men a day
come to the tip
for the scavenging,
prospectors of rubbish,
sifters of trash,
scrabbling for what
the bulldozers churn,
unwanted transistors
scrap iron and rags,
thrown-away men
in a throw-away world.

The scavengers
on Bidston Tip
dive like the gulls
for other men's scraps,
the discarded offal
of obsolete junk,
yesterday's ovens,
technology's trash,
other folks' anoraks,
trousers and shoes,
bike frames and fridges,
lost rings and pens,
jackets, cheap jewellery,
misplaced tomfoolery,
men on a scrapheap.
A scrapheap of men.

Geoff Fenwick

THE BOX

I want to reach right in,
put my hand through the glass
and pull him from the desert,
but you have sealed tight the box
with the frame of your lens,
and run with his image
like a diamond shifted from
the sands of opportunity.
The plane is waiting,
it takes you to the spolit stage
where they crown your triumph,
and sweating with the heat of their applause
you hold up your treasure,
this parchment man,
stripped to the bone by the famine
of our ignorance.

Perhaps on Sunday afternoon,
when they have cleared the table
and you finish your Bordeaux
by the glow of the fire,
you will mount him on the wall,
just so,
and normalise his horror
in the soft-peach decor
of your livingroom.

Jane MacNamee

TERRITORIES

In the stillness of the park
two black cats stare out their confrontation;
one shaped as if a semicolon,
the other a feline fullstop.

Only a magpie and I saw this

between hearing dribs and drabs
of other conflicts, blazing from FM News.

Their eyes burnt through each other's
as if this were some final conflict
between two Marvel superheroes.
But no-one else saw.

And when one sat - and lolled in the grass,
the other padded away.

The magpie left as a dove then

As if they'd learnt to shake paws
- and let it run another day.

Alan M Kent

ELEPHANT ETERNITY

Elephants walking under juicy-leaf trees
Walking with their children under juicy-leaf trees
Elephants, elephants walking like time

Elephants bathing in the foam-floody river
Fountaining their children in the motherly river
Elephants, elephants bathing like happiness

> Strong and gentle elephants
> Standing on the earth
> Strong and gentle elephants
> Like peace

Time is walking under elephant trees
Happiness is bathing in the elephant river
Strong, gentle peace is shining
All over the elephant earth.

Adrian Mitchell

UNTITLED

In a frail seclusion zone.
All of them gathered
around you.
They whimpered,
whilst they stared.
Gazes upon high
no cry
could be heard.
They closed you in,
bearing their weight
heavily upon your skin.
Beaten up.

Lucy Williams

PLACE OF THE WATER:
FOR ALL THOSE WHO TOGETHER MAKE A WELL.

No worry these days,
no hurry, now
I am happy-headed
walking out this way
this old way
this familiar long snake-winding
way under the big-faced
sun. And he, smiling down
at me, at the swinging
of my hips and the sway
making rhythm with the beat
of my feet
feather-feathering the earth
slip-slapping at the hot sand
scuffing on the
pearly pebbles of the dry-bed
river, winding on down
to the place of the water.

And its down-rope dipping
snaking deep in the dark
with the dripping pitcher
lifting skywards cool and high:
fine feathered water bird
sleek and damp in the black
moss-bank of my hair - then home
upon wings.

Marilyn Carter

F WORDS

The baboons stared
surprised in their mutual
search for parasites.
I enquired
in a search of my own
and answering
the keeper dismissed them
with a brief reference.

'They display,' he said
'the usual obsessions of
captive primates,
feeding, fighting,'
he paused for effect,
'and fornicating.'

I forgot the baboons
and all that was said
until just today
reading the press
when I found that the news
could be neatly compressed into

feeding, fighting, fornicating,

and not much else.

J P Portlock

FACTORY - FRAGMENT FROM A DIARY

Beware! Forklift trucks turning
Asbestos roofing - Unsafe
Breathing air - wear masks
Liquid nitrogen, no smoking
Dangerous chemicals.

Dead seals lie on a nearby beach
and decay in the sun.
Flies buzz in and out of the black blood -
Sunday beach memories.

On Monday the rotting plastic smells
invade my thought again.
Twelve redundancies after the summer
Safety levels maintained
Maximum profits.
How many minds are reeling?
Body fluids congealing?

Come Friday . . . burn the factory to the ground,
let the embers by the statement of my love.

Ian Duckett

GRUDGEMENTS

(To be cut out and enclosed with donations to charities)
i
My bank will verify that I exist,
But please don't add me to your mailing-list:
The circulars I get on every question
Have made me spin with mental indigestion.
ii
No mailings, please. It don't seem right,
Whatever cause it's for,
That you should spend the widow's mite
On asking her for more.

iii
(For the charity which rang to ask people chosen from the phone
book for help with door-to-door collections during
its week, the money to be paid in at local banks)
iv
From the Cyrenians, maybe,
How resonantly it would speak,
This asking strangers such as me
To go the extra mile one week!
From others, though, whether or not you like it,
The cheek is what strikes most, and here I strike it.

(For any charity dealing with homelessness, physical or mental
illness, prison, or senile decay)

It's not a gift. If my life's hit,
It's all I could afford -
I hope you will remember it,
And treat me as insured.

Aidan Baker

CHARITY BEGINS AT HOME

'An appeal was made for the dying
In another country, not our own.'
'Die they must, it's not my problem,
I'd rather save lives closer to home.'

'A fund is open for the needy,
In our country, yes our home.'
'I'm not paying to feed the greedy,
It's their problem, theirs alone.'

'It's the boss' birthday, you know,
And a party's being planned for the rat.'
'Here's a tenner for his present,
Didn't have to think twice about that.'

Suman Ghosh

FINDING HIS FEET
This poem is dedicated to Dr P K Sethi who invented the Jaipur Limb

At eighteen
had he known
that he was the person they meant
when they said antipersonnel
would he have stayed
within bounds?

Afterwards he showed no gift for becoming
a statistic: one of the hundreds
of paper amputees
each month claimed.

He sat slumped in
no pained corners.
As the stumps healed
though unevenly, he knew
that what remained
of his heavenly body
must move.

Clasped by the beaten metal
sheaths, he finds his feet,
rubbered to take the strain.

Two bars now for a road,
he is back on track:
Jaipur limbing-it
along the parallel pathway
to a self-determined day.

Don Patter

HAIKU

1994
John, Paul, George and Ringo seem
so irrelevant.

Anthony Cox

BACK IN THE NINETIES

Back in the nineties fears I chose not to see
sneaked down peacetime streets I didn't even know.

Prickles, as hot as shrapnel, on the nape of my neck
now rise in memory of my walking past
those stark niches
of shut shop doorways cradling the arrogant homeless;
who encroached on us like foreign colonials
with their cardboard beds and angry sleeping-bags.
Could they have been waiting?
Did they know?

Now as I lie here amongst my home's broken bricks
my government has become sniper-fire and distant thuds.
I obey the rules of warfare - you have to,
they can't be broken.

'Just nipping down to the standpipe, dear.' - I quip
and wince with stiff lip to the numb ghost
of my sniper-raped wife.

The incendiary glare of realisation shimmers
in my bombed out head that used to wear a bowler.
I remember the newspaper stand that used to be
outside Sainsbury's on our High Street:
a discreet beacon of that sneaking fear
speaking of tragedies I never believed in
- like that far-off, war-ripped country
that used to be a holiday resort in Europe.

They took Leicester last week;
already they're bombing Watford.
We all know the capital will fall to the rebels.

The rebels?
But aren't they Englishmen just like me?

Mark A Goodwin

RAIN

Rain
that does not fall alike on whom
it falls nor falls
on everyone and every place
but chooses its
gross abundance or scarcity
by place, season
or sheer power of mystery,
extravagance
and a curiosity lost
in capricious
questioning of how we handle
both excesses,
which we do not well. Plenty breeds
its wastefulness
and inadequacy
despair,
selfishness and
a *what I get, I have, and keep*
that only trusts
the having now and keeping all.

Having breeds an
unfamiliarity with need
and contrary
experience habituates
an attitude
that blinds the eyes that might have seen
and stops the ears
that might have known the cries that die
for want and need
of watering of seeds of care
where waters flow
abundantly to irrigate
and bring empathy to flower.

A K Whitehead

THERE ARE TIMES

Stark photographs beckon me along dark, fetid tracks,
Pitifully scraped by a million cholera-stricken refugees,
To a desperate, dubious place, a position of parallax,
A coexistence with victims of war, famine and disease.

There are times when I share the captured torment,
When I understand the reality, the black and the white,
I can see this world, our excuses and the extent
of your anger, the horror, the depth of your insight.

On the photographs of Don McCullin

Richard Gallie

GALLOWS IN MY EYES (AN APOLOGY FOR APATHY)

I suppose you think that I should seem concerned
I guess you feel that I should seem to care
It might bleed in black and white
From the pages that I read
But if I close my eyes
It appears not to be there

I hold a finger up to catch direction of the breeze
But an ill-wind blows both ways these days I find
But there you are, you tell me how to feel
Perhaps you gave some pennies to a national appeal?
There's no reason to expect anymore than you will get
So I ask you to refrain from casting blame

In a tombstone instant, there's gallows in my eyes
But I don't raise a finger
And I refuse to reason why
In a tombstone instant, there's gallows in my eyes
But I don't

Stuart Elden

TO CHANGE MY MIND

There is a richness of resources
To which I feel a birthright.
But, *right* of birth -
Does that bestowal assign to me and mine
What history has determined as a level of contentment,
With margins in excess of need?
My place of birth has brought me privilege,
What in another place, another circumstance
Would count as an outrageous opulence.
And I decide, and I divide the *them* and *us,*
And by my wants condemn who should and who should not possess,
Defined by culture, creed, or class;
Or simply, turn my back on those not of *our sort.*

There is a poverty in my resources,
And in my vision, to see that, as with Shakespeare's Ulysses,
'One touch of nature makes the whole world kin.'
So may my richness be that sight -
That insight to perceive the obligation
That goes beyond the guilt-spurred, cold compassion:
My poverty of thought and action now be turned
To rich engagement in the War on Want,
And be that fight a constant part of me.

Don Reeve

DOUBLE CHECK

I check you out
in the light provided
by the dawn sky

the blues, greys and yellows
the whites, greens and browns
of your eyes

the cut
of your teeth

your body punctured
with sleep
hope
and forgetfulness

I check
and double check

but still I remember
old radios playing
food and drink left out
arrangements to come back
and all those people starving.

Mark Blackmore

OCTOBER WOODS

The forest floor - mud underfoot - leaves its mark
up Jessica's sodden legs and flanks,
evidence of the passing of horses and foxes
is smeared with joy on Jessie's neck.

I sit on cut and piled trunks - mainly beech -
stacked on the forest floor, and the sun's dapple
comes and goes on bramble undergrowth
jewelled with conkers and raindrops.

New plantings are swaddled within plastic tubes,
protective and inhibiting as the old familiar nurse.
The tubes are ranked and angled away as though
a cross reference to World War One cemeteries.

The adult trees show sixty feet of twisted, naked trunk
to their canopy of branches that supports the usual mix -
dark leaves almost black against blue and white sky,
and the canopies of other trees leaning drunkenly.

Michael Facherty

HOW MANY FALLEN HEROES?

How many fallen heroes
have their echoes in this
dear child?

Shadows,
raging water,
splish-splash

the rain hits the sides of the
gorge like a knock at the door
which is like a knock at the
heart

the rain rolls down gullies and
rills,
each one carefully constructed
by the small ingenious
hands of a
story.

A story in the landscape.

The landscape which is dizzy
grey with the dreamscape

which is most certainly the
heartscape
of yet another fallen hero,
lying on a back broken
by imagination.

Staring at the depths of the tapestry
that is the sky.
The sky above a landscape or
a dreamscape.

It doesn't matter.

Daniel Etherington

MIND

I want to go inside she screamed.

And what about you? What do you want to do?

I want to slice my hand
On the neck of a broken bottle
To smear my face, my neck

And the grass.
To cut my fingers razor-sharp.

I want to open my mouth
And have a lizard come out of it

Piped up the one right at the back.
How odd we thought
But I understood what she meant
Imagine if all your insides got caught in its tail
Then the rest of you would come out too

I wonder if that makes me weird?
Someone at the heart of the matter
Said I want to go home
I wonder if you can eat yourself?
If you start biting bits off (maybe use a meat cleaver for the harder bits)
And swallowing them
Then you'd be able to get inside yourself
That would be quite nice too.

She sometimes managed to escape into sleep
But sleep brought morning nearer
And the mornings were the worst -
Afraid of thinking up something new

They all held hands
Some gently, some firmly
And some dug their nails in.

I want to go inside she screamed.
E A Mottershaw

UNTITLED

Like a large wet sack of sand
His body squashed itself in its own weight
And was impossible to write

Cold
Stiff
Stank like blood from a half-thawed Christmas turkey
And where my fingers pressed it in
Flesh slipped slowly back on a half-forgotten path

Inoffensive - death
Eyes and mouth half-opened as he died
As if to mock himself in a mute angelic pose

He never acted better
His designer-kitsch never dared as far
As the plastic bag that wrapped him up

Nothing to fear
It didn't moan or groan or leap to bite my throat
But lay and rotted
Stuffed with cottonwool against the leak

Not so much a life snuffed out
As drained away in three long years
Until it came to be that death
Was the more attractive choice

And so I kiss him
Kiss it
Smooth the hair
And stay awhile
Make it real
And say goodbye.

Jon Pyper

HUMAN RIGHTS BEGIN WITH BREAKFAST

Human rights begin with breakfast
And if I could just get across
This road without being shot.
Through that minefield without being blown-up
I'd eat the breakfast the plane dropped.

Human rights begin with breakfast
If I wait long enough
Perhaps it'll rain
And I can plant these seeds
And might even eat bread; one day.

Human rights begin with breakfast
Perhaps if I'm very good, very quiet
If I don't annoy them
After I've cleaned the house, done the washing,
Mummy might let me have a slice of bread.

Human rights begin with breakfast
Yes, they do, for all these people
Tripping over my feet, in my house
As they go to work, grumbling
I'd be happy to do their work, for a square meal.

Human rights begin with breakfast
What rights? I'm black, and gay
I'm lucky they let me live
Huddled in the damp, dark, cold, hard floor,
Perhaps I'll catch a rat for dinner; more likely a cockroach.

Human rights begin with breakfast
Kidney and kedgeree, eggs and bacon
Toast, marmalade; coffee, hot, fresh.
Millionaires feast over news
of famine, war homelessness; fed up.

Angie Gold

STRENGTH

Each insignificant piece of us,
Watch the sandstorm,
Watch;
Army of many arms and legs.
Just dust.
As it flows across the land,
We trudge through the sand.
Walk in desperation
Walk through humiliation
Walk to the destination
You steal our roots
Bleed us dry
Your clichés will not dry
Our eyes;
One day a speck of grit
Will alight upon your eye,
And all your sins you will
Remember.

Nuzhat Jabinh (17)

SKIN DEEP

Rain dribbles of racism seep into society,
splattering hard against the panes of resistance.
Easier to conform and to talk of the cultural divide,
than to face the enemy within.
Easier to point a finger at the different Other,
than to change from inside.
For rain is only wet when it touches the skin,
when the body is exposed to the elements.
So, stay inside, keep dry, and close both eyes.
Then there simply isn't a problem.

Alison Hill

LONDON LADY

She lies crumpled for support
Against a dark December
Weeping in the late city,
Almost hidden as you pass
Her back to the wall
Damp and grey as slate
Harder than the wind
Through the ancient railing gates.
She disturbs you for a second
This Euvydice in vagrant mask
Staring blindly out of Hades,
while you walk more quickly home.
You hope she's gone tomorrow
But she will still be there
Her moment life beside the gates
A small statue of rags
Just briefly looked upon.

Robert Galer

SIMPLE DESPERATION

I'm really not happy,
It's time to be true,
I'm so terribly scared,
I really don't know what to do.

I don't know what I want,
I don't know where to go,
What will make me happy?
I really do not know.

I don't know who to turn to,
I feel there's no-one there,
So I pretend I don't need anyone,
Because I know that no-one cares.

Pip G Fitzpatrick

DEVASTATION

I am writing this poem on trees:
Trees that once grew tall,
Greening the view with beauty,
Holding the soil.

And now? - Now all that is left
Is a bare-boned hillside,
Raked by channelled claws,
Where rain flashed off in a flood,
Removing fertility in rushing roar
To choke the plains with mud.

Half a millennium ago
I would have written this poem on a calf:
Big-eyed, brown-eyed beauty,
Dying too young - and yet
The herd would reproduce
Endless vellum for our use;
At least till we cut the forest down,
And the pastures died
Then, no more hide!

Elizabeth Grantham

REFUGEES

When do we leave -
Cancel the milk, stop the papers?
There are whispers on the train
And letters go astray.
We are not wanted here.

Once we were decent folk,
Growing a little stout,
Respecting the law and the neighbours.
We cast our vote, when we remembered,
And forgot it decently afterwards.

Now waiters refuse to serve us
And the school has no places.
The man on the street shouts hate
Not news, and our parties are invaded
By black-shirted men.

Perhaps we should pack our cases.
But where should we go? And how?
The wind blows cold across the station.
Who would want us anyway -
Decent folk, growing a little stout?

Pauline Kirk

LETTER FROM THE NURSING HOME

You must forgive me, for I am not entirely grown up yet.
I bang and hit the table when nurses pass
(whispering just a second, Mrs P, be with you in a minute),
running wheelchairs round my feet.

I bang and call, rocking in my rage
at loss of beauty's power;
age instead has left me blind, incontinent,
inhabitant of lonely, shrunken mind.

I bang and clutch the crusted garment of my life -
crying within, without,
O God, where were you when I need most
to lose my breath before I grew like this?

O God, forgive those younger than myself
who purge with pills and call me dear, a child -

I rage and bang: there's nothing left to lose
for dignity, like love, is seldom here.

Death, and only death, is left to fear
and nightly tiptoes by
cuddling compassion, now my woolly toy.

Maeve Reid

COME MY GREAT PATRIOT

People have starved to death,
too many to the square mile.
Come my dear Behemoth,
surely that once made you smile?

And many disintegrated
for strange political reasons.
No-one knows where they went, but dead
they no longer offer treasons.

And others will be shot
too stupid to reconcile.
Come my great patriot,
surely that will make you smile?

Eric Nixon

UNITED NATIONS' BUILDING

Here in multistoreys with acres of glass
Where all the tribes meet
A big man pronounces.
With two thousand missiles under his seat
We listen with respect.

A small man rises, bows politely
And makes a telling point.
Backed by a strong economy
He is poised, self-assured
And we listen with respect.

A distinguished, elder statesman
In slightly shabby suit
But dignified, unflappable,
Familiar with the broker's role
Takes a balanced view
And we listen with respect.

A thin, dark man
With a humble voice
Speaks quietly of his people's needs,
Of those who having little choice
Must stand and watch while children starve.
Help us survive he pleads
And we listen uncomfortably.

Ron Woollard

BUILDING BRIDGES

Long ago, a river divided
two lands, and the people
who lived on one side of the river
wondered what it would be like on the other.
It was different, they knew that,
harsher and wilder
and beyond it were places and people
they'd only heard of.

In time, a bridge was built,
founded on an act of torture.
Over the centuries, armies marched
across the bridge to occupy the city,
lovers whispered under it, poets
dreamed of it, philosophers
argued about it, fools fooled on it
and children played.

If bridges were not built
life might be simpler
but when they are, they bring the stranger
who sometimes chooses to stay for ever
to share in the land's history
and be part of its richness
now handed on to generations
of children who come after.

Cicely Herbert

SORRY SOULS

I salved my conscience at twelve o'clock today.
I saw a man standing quietly in the street.
His clothes were shabby, worn and old
And yet he smiled at me, though said no word.

It cost me just a pound to buy his magazine.
It must have cost him more to sell his wares:
It cost him time and pride to take such stares
From the passing rich, intent on Christmas shopping.

It was not hard for me to proffer money
Just as a helpless witness would proffer hands.
I did it because I heard his face
And felt remorse that we both share
Such a place as this.

Calum Miller

SRI LANKA - MAY 1992
A visit to a Plantation Line House

She beamed with delight
And offered a cup of muddy water
To quench a stranger's thirst

She was small
For her eleven years
But reminded me of a loved one

The muddy water
Smelled of well-trampled earth
And burnt wood
And as I drank
it scratched its way down my throat

'Why cry?'
She asked, as tears rolled down my face
And looked at me with an innocence
That reminded me of a loved one

'The water,' I said
'It scratched my throat.'

Her eyes fixed on me for a second time
And a small part of her innocence
Disappeared for ever

For she knew
As I knew

The water
It had scratched my heart.

Stephen Faulkner

YOUR BILL

over the edge of the knife of hunger
exists another world
beyond the locus of love songs
are torments devised by pol pot,
amin, da vinci, hitler, croesus
over the edge & beyond the capacity of poetry
worlds
in which sparrow chirps are irrelevant
worlds in which
all my words would decay
where none of my formulae would be valid
worlds in which it wouldn't matter
if your painting disintegrated
or if your symphony was ever composed
the only music here
the scream
the moan
and finally the silence
the manifesto of the dying child

Jacob Bush

LIBERTY ISLAND - NEW YORK

We gave you our sick, our tired, our lonely
Our hungry, our homeless, our poor
Our weary, our desolate ones
I have seen them on your subways
In your parks, on the corners of your streets
With their paper cups, rattling coins
Under their newspapers
Carrying their plastic bags
Drinking from dirty bottles
Scavenging the garbage
While here you stand in majesty
Safe across the water
Where money is needed to visit freedom.

I am no better than you
I stand as silent
As straight, as unseeing
Holding the torch of my own liberty
Wearing my crown of the civilised
Bearing my book of morality, yet somehow
Not knowing our gifts to you, who remain
As sick, as tired, as lonely
As hungry, as homeless, as poor
As weary, as desolate
As human as I, Miss Liberty
Or you.

John Dougherty

ONE QUESTION

I want to give up being a bullet
I've been a bullet too long

I want to be an innocent coin
in the hand of a child
and be squeezed through the slot
of a bubblegum machine

I want to give up being a bullet
I've been a bullet too long

I want to be a good-luck seed
lying idle in somebody's pocket
in some ordinary little stone
on the way to becoming an earring
our just lying there unknown
among a crowd of other ordinary stones
I want to give up being a bullet
I've been a bullet too long

The question is
Can you give up being a killer?

John Agard

JUST A SPADE

The man walked out of the desert.
He carried his child on his back.
Death stalked them both like a shadow,
desolate, wasted and black.
They came to a refugee city,
where tents stretched, mile upon mile.
'We have built you a great cathedral,'
the do-gooders said, with a smile.

The man looked up at the building,
towering over his head.
He thought of his starving children,
'I just need a spade,' he said.
'I do not want a cathedral . . .
With a spade I could bury my dead.
I could dig for the life giving waters.
Please, give me a spade instead.'

Judith P Powe

UNTITLED

Smooth sleep . . .
Drifting, calm, safely warm,
Cloaked, embraced by false reality
The twenty-year-old child awakes,
Eyes crumpled at the sun,
She stares.
Light dawns on marble head.
Pulls the cloak tighter,
Turns to sleep,
Sleep,
Sleep to escape.

R D Murray

CRISIS IN AFRICA

Our food is but a dusty bowl,
From God his gift for life;
Each night you sit and view the whole,
These bones are still my wife.

I long for death to rescue us,
My child to join the truck,
A mobile grave, a freedom bus
So Auschwitz like - good luck!

I hear of things quite possible,
Transport and surplus grain,
We cling to life without the will
To cry for help from pain.

Goodbye until your Lord he comes;
You're certain that he will?
I'll shake your hand with my new limbs,
And save you from all ill.

D Carter

WIDE EYES

Wide eyes on glass
staring, blind
seeing nothing.

Wide eyes in TV,
weeping child
famine tied.

Starvation.
Death.
Violence unkind.
Fucked.
Untouched
the anaesthetised mind.

Cry eyes criminal,
iceberg heart
coldness inside.

Genocide.
Greed.
Castrating lies.
Protest.
Sense
the batons rise.

Cry eyes stupid,
controlled rage
burning outside.

Cried eyes witness
falling land.

Switching channel,
complacent hand.

David Golledge

METAMORPHOSIS

The point
Has been missed;
Her point.
Heartfelt love
Lost to you.
How can it be
That an angel
Metamorphoses
Into a stone?
Understand it all,
Should she?
You prick pain
In her strength
With the pin
Of underestimation
Of her true worth.
You have far
To travel on
Before you see
She weeps for you,
Not for herself.

Solomon Blue-Waters

THE ROVER AND THE BLANKET

The temple is the workplace:
The holy grail the bank.
The pilgrims stand and ponder by the door.
The *Situations vacant* mask the face of *other-abled* -
Our euphemisms mock us by the score.

To Habitat and B&Q and envy in the car park
We flock anew each Sunday morning fresh.
We offer up our plastic with its hologram of promise,
And pray it's buying work for other flesh.

Our fear shines through our hub caps.
We pay to keep them rolling.
We hope thereby that nobody will see
That Pharisees are packing self-build kitchens in the Rover:
That homeless pavement blanket could be me.

Wendy Hill

CUBA LIBRE

Oil fires burn in the clouds
orange fingers of flame and developer's cranes'
curved backs draw question marks
in a cheap Chinese restaurant dish sky.

The familiar black Mercedes glides by: men in blacked-out glasses
behind blacked-out windows. An old man is moving down the beach
his pace stately as a 1930s Ocean liner. In the distance the pink
cupolas of *Las Americas,* the former DuPont mansion
flutter in the wind alongside the breasts of German women
floating by like apparitions. 'Truth is for tourists,' laugh the *marecons*
just out of prison. Their hipless grace scythes the evening
slicing it on the cusp between beauty and starvation. I too grew
                                            up on an island
where you stayed only if you could eat scenery. Last night
I had a dream: I was trapped on that island, its blue mountains
had a thousand mouths which consumed my passport
its coasts were spiked with beasts and oil slicks, with the
                                            MININT men
who say, 'Welcome to Cuba,' but who don't say goodbye.

Some believe that to know hunger
you must forsake food. Women haven't had chicken
in a year. River-blindness has struck, its gauzy cataracts
gutting the eyelids. And every night
the gut of this blue whale-shaped country
comes closer to turning breadfruit to flesh
and rum to blood.

Jean McNeil

SLOW DEATH

Congratulations, charming stranger
you have succeeded
where all else has failed
to bring me to my knees
pleading for mercy
for the torture to stop
I have been strong
during many trials
duplicities, double-dealings
trusting in the gods
and my wild nature
to see me thru'

You, having raised me up
to allow glimpses
of a better world,
of how it could be,
not just sacrifice, subsistence
and survival, but health, hope,
and dare I say it, happiness
then snatched it away
with a cruel, cold, 'Sorry'.
Now it's even too late
for me to die with dignity

Adrienne Lewis

18TH CENTURY : RE-VISITED

Star date : 18th Century
Red Jackets march off to war
To unknown land of *savages*
Fighting for King and Country;
Spreading the British word
Natives stand no chance
Another possession for The Empire.

Star date : 1994
Multi-national closes in
Savages need our help!
Help means baby milk;
Spread the Western word
Colonialism in all but name
Profit thrives on misery.

Star date : 21st Century
Vision of the future
Savages rise triumphant
Over corpse of multi-national;
Exploitation at an end
Third World rising
What the West's afraid of?

Truth; justice; equality;
The New World Order.

Jon Hopper

TABOO

Indoors the corridors I walk
Are laid in mosaic mistrust
Whispers pass for talk
And I have learnt to fear the dust
That falls from other men's shoes.

And I would sit beneath
A hawthorn tree
And I would only breathe
The perfume between it and me

Remembering the old taboo
That carried with it the yaboo
Omen of bad luck for those who broke
The hawthorn branch and tried to yoke
Its magic to a world indoors.

Eilish Martin

DUST TRAIL TO CALVARY

After all - it's nice to have nice things.
If I had my wish I'd look good-looking
Like good-looking men who don't ever think
But just wear the same old stink
Yet look like the best you can bring.

It's nice to have nice things, after all;
Sweat, eyes, teeth, limbs, gall
Fitted on so as to make the best of all
'Cos I'm slightly worn out - actually
From the lack of nice things, factually;

Like an outing, a meal without residuals,
A day without divisions, an unblocked annual,
A ladderless life without snakes and strain,
This constant going against the grain,
No let-up from lugging on a lead-weight mammal.

Jesus once lived and flared. How warm
The wind of welcome rushing through Jerusalem.
Three lousy days in an early anno domini spring
Then an eternity of nice things.
I'm coming off the rails so cross my beams.

In times gone by these limbs were golden,
This sweat scented with spice cones* waxen,
These eyes dusted with powdered seed,
Pith glistened in between these teeth,
And I had the gall to ignore you.

P G McCormack
*In ancient Egypt scented cones were placed on party-goers heads.

PATIENCE II

I am the face of the hedgerow
the ear of the being sky
the eye of the silent crackling sun.
I am the piece of you
you forgot to remember.

Bound in thought and thinking ways
you trace a clever path
but I am always here
Simple and simply being
and ever present
I do not think
I am beyond thought
Beyond all things - I am all things.
I am the throbbing pulse of the granite
deep below the burning stubble of your daily ways
far beneath your beautiful tiny feet
as they race their complex wearying routine

I am the voice that guides you
the voice you over-ride
the voice that makes no sound
but resounds about you and feeds your being

I am the stillness within
you fear to embrace
The silence you shun for more exciting ways
The resting place your many strivings block

I am here and I am everywhere
and I am nowhere
and this I will always be

Julian Sharples

TREELESSNESS

They bartered their trees for the taste of money
four seasons later, burned by the sun, they squeezed their
                                          bottles last drop.
Their land slept refusing to grow, their berries hardened quickly
                                                          into raisins,
their houses slipped off the slopes, the diarrhetic land washing
                                                             them away.

The mysterious paper astounded them
more so than the breadth of a copper harvest moon,
the coloured flutter of a flock of startled birds
the flecks of gold at the bottom of a deep stream pool.

It was simply shavings of patterned bleached bark, but the
                                                  power of exchange . . .
so thick and rich, the liquid, so slender and smooth, the bottle
such signs and shapes on the labels, there was another world
                                                      there to discover
beyond the stubbled forest which was their own.

But without their trees, birds don't perch
without birds, insects thrive
with many insects the plants are quickly devoured
without the plants the dwellings can't be built
people grow ill and the medicinal plants are infested or dry
or no longer grow because without trees
the environment tilts out of balance.

The chief was handed one hundred papers, as the trees
                                                were felled, hauled away.
There is so much sky and there is so much sun
but thick trees don't grow back in a year.
And when the last paper is surrendered the loggers are long gone
while the tribe must move, die or dissolve for their sins.

Emily Marbach

THE PROBLEM WITH THE WORLD TODAY

The problem with the world today
Is it's full of people like me
Who live in sheltered, cosy homes
And only see war on TV.

The problem with the world today
Is it's full of people like him
People whose world may be blasted apart
By some feuding commander's whim.

The problem with the world today
Is it's full of people like me
Who stand around at parties
And discuss what it means to be free.

The problem with the world today
Is it's full of people like her
People who dared voice an opinion
And were tortured for how foolish they were.

The problem with the world today
Is it's full of people like me
Who talk about revolution
From the comfort of a paisley settee.

The problem with the world today
Is it's full of people like him
Who try to organise workers groups
But are murdered in the interim.

The problem with the world today
Is it's full of people like us
We know it's all wrong, but our world's okay,
So why should we kick up a fuss?

Marina Gaze

ALL STAFF

Please see the following,

> Seminars have been scheduled
> To help you meet your deadlines!
> Situations to be managed include:
>
> - Basic Humanity
> - Value Systems
> - Effort vs Worth (workshop)
>
> To encourage you to consider these issues
> Any performance bonus will be based on attendance.
>
> Profits aren't measured; even in nos. of zeros.
> No overtime will be paid.
>
> Key drivers* will be
>
> - Self Motivation,
> - Ethics Evaluation
> - Competition Assessment.
>
> The agendas are full of Any Other Business.

Due to the importance of these events
To the overall strategy of the infinite
Your support would be appreciated.

No papers attached.
Previous Corporate Directives
(eg Satisfaction of the Brighter or the Luckier
ie Those Who Set The Timetable)
(see Key Processes for Improvement)
Do not apply to these events.

David Topliff

INHERITANCE

      Unmarked the moment when our fathers lost
man's innocence to automated killing.
The prisoners' feet were kissed by winter frost,
their hunger ached. Some opted out, unwilling
to stumble on with pride and will run out.

They deemed a small delay a meagre prize,
fell gently and remained there calm and solemn,
unless one were to shout at them to rise,
awaiting death behind the marching column.
And some men had the stubborn strength to shout.

      They've left to us the throb of phantoms' feet
and monuments esteemed by every nation,
a world of wealthy customers to eat
the feast of plenty set by automation -
and now and then a fearful, halting doubt

when warplanes scrape across the sky a scar
above our loved ones' heads or when the telly
brings for our entertainment from afar
a child with hunger bloated in the belly
and we have lost the voice or will to shout.

Thomas Land

ME AND YOU

Give to me, give to me!
But I cannot give.
Take from me, take from me!
But I cannot take.
Leave me, leave me!
But I cannot leave you.

David Whatley

I AM

I am the rainbow haze around the moon on a still night . . .
The twittering of starlings as the nuclear train disturbs
their nesting . . .
I am an angry bundle of expanding atoms that wants to live
on my Mother planet and smell the jasmine after rain, and
know that I will always smell that smell . . .
I am a potential compost heap that one day will make
carrots grow . . .
I am the tears of a battered woman . . .
I am the audience at a Feminist Poetry Reading that turns and
stares at the *Lads at the Back* but doesn't have a bag of
Poodle turds to throw at them . . .
I am the tear from a child's eye when its mother has no
milk in an arid desert made so by the destruction of a million
trees . . .
I am the planter of seeds and Rose Crystals to save the Earth . . .
I am the anger turned to love, the giver of good vibrations
no matter what.

Karen Jorgensen

THE CHILDREN IN ANGOLA

Served by a waiter, fresh fish and wine,
With invited friends we've come to dine,
The sunset glows, what a tranquil scene,
While the rollers sweep the beaches clean.

Relaxed, we don't see, those haunted eyes,
Of children who search bins with hungry cries,
Eager to eat the food we discard,
By Angola's war their bodies scarred.

We do not wince at their fleshless ribs,
Or see the burnt child in a row of cribs,
Or the thousands of others that queue to eat,
Or a boy battered for a fruit, on our city street.

These young lives, have known only the war,
Their parents lay still, they'll move no more,
One without crutches, mourns in a hospital ward,
But our eyes remain on this sumptuous board.

Janet E Greenyer

HATE POEM

You gently take her from her sleep
And pull her into darkened rooms
Drag her down into the depths
Where Satan rots and you betray
Her ornamental innocence
Her chastity, her wide-eyed charm
One plunge and she cannot be cleansed
See Katie's soul disintegrate
See every grain of trust she bore
Crack and crumble, fall and die
Her soft devotion, reverence
She held you high, unknowingly
With every touch feel Katie quake
Know her heart no longer beats
Taste her blood, so cold, now marred
Drown in rivers from her eyes
No more a child but ages old
She stands, like Eve, with fruit in hand
But passively, for you're to blame
Her tiny body now decays
So go, and leave her, used and bruised
You have no guilt, you cannot mend
The tiny spirit you have crushed
A shame your hands won't be displayed
Bloodstained for all the world to see.

Sara Whitmarsh

EXILES

We're blue like babies
cold like fishes out of water
tangled as stitches in thin air.

There's no reason in us.
No heart . . . no home . . . no hearth.

Figures on a shattered vase
grooves on a mill stone
blood on a rag.

Jenny Vuglar

LOST

Menacing, in the deserted distance
    Sunday in Spitalfields market
    Deserted

They grouped soldier like
    Wagon train like
    Around the fire
Facing outwards

I had to pass them
    On my way to Liverpool Street,
And a million people
    And the east of England
    And the world.

Would they attack
    This hostile group
These no-hopers

I passed few feet away
    They didn't see me
    I dared to look at each
    There was no group

Only twelve dying men
    On their cold feet
Warming their backs
    Against death.

James O'Grady

OVER HERE

Whatever happened to fascism?
How come Hitler didn't get a grip?
Why wasn't freethinking freedom daunted?
What was it caused that war?
Nationalism?

Why didn't it happen here? - It did
It still is
Why wasn't it roused as much in Britain
It was - xenophobia - primitive wisdom -
Brown-shirts - Mosley
Basic instincts - nationalism
What stopped it? - Nazism did

The first bomb Hitler dropped - stopped
What was just as rife in Britain?
Did you realise - what happened at the
Old Trafalgar - in the East End?
It was the end of this the meeting place
Of these the English fascists - eighty of them
Leaders - busy planning right-wing rising
Just one bomb away from
Fascism happening here

I wish we could say that now it's not
But at least that first of Hitler's raids
Dropped on the Old Trafalgar
And killed the bloody lot.

Adrian Spendlow

FED UP!

'Jus wern meur waffer theen meent, Monsieur!'
I tease myself and then I stuff another four,
And, just in case indulgence were to soon go out of date,
I reach across and choose another biscuit from the plate;
Then with a flick of wrist I activate the TV set,
To watch the film on BBC I hope's not started yet.
I'm irritated by the News that's coming to me live
From those abroad that went and caused the fuss in '85.
Then, poverty was *sexy* and championed by the stars;
It even had its own theme tune, written by *The Cars*.
That image though has seemed to, well, weary some of late
And so I go and choose another biscuit from the plate.
But skins and bones; and flies and tears: They all begin to gnaw,
Subconsciously, to make you dwell on misery some more . . .
And more . . . And more . . . And more . . .
On Famine and Starvation; on Hunger and the Poor.
Then Tyranny and Torture; then Conflict and then Wars;
Then, ultimately, helplessness and hopelessness of cause.
So, guiltily, I pledge to find some money to donate,
To purge my selfish feelings and I find an empty plate.
So, absently, I pledge to buy some biscuits from the store,
As I look and see those wafer mints:
                'Oh, go on 'jus wern meur.'
Peter Shenlack

DESTINY

Look to the future,
  'What do you see?'
Rainforests,
  Without a tree.

Irreparable damage,
  From polluted air,
Caused by people,
  Who don't really care.

Smoke from our factories,
    Waste dumped in the sea.
Less fish in the water,
    Fewer birds, in the tree.

Please think ahead,
    It's our children's fate.
Take action now,
    Before, it's too late.

Betty Elliott

PARTY POLITICS

Live to excess
Try to find success
Speak quickly
Lie rapidly

Do not be afraid of hate
Stay in a corrupt state
Run away
Dodge people to keep them at bay

Drink don't think
Hold principles that stink
Appear to defend them with all your might
But remember to forget to fight

Never give but sell
Invest wisely as well
Money is everything
Cheating is worth considering

Above all keep everybody guessing
By doing nothing.

Stephen Neal

NEW YORK, NEW YORK

New York, new york:
familiar backdrop
to seasons of TV street scenes;
Mona Lisa
      with acne;
Big Apple riddled to the core
with the 20th Century worm;
Liberty's lamp
      and the beggar's paper-cup;
cars, long and luxurious
      as hearses;
the American dream
blown with the paper on 42nd Street,
or hiding in trash-cans,
foraged for
      by down-and-outs.

Alan Manford

UNTITLED

My eyes are closed, inward turned.
The black and grey of sleep won't rest tonight.
Shapes rise and fall,
Contorting in an agony of birth and death,
Spectral images, felt, not seen, yet are.
Tormenting concepts of form that could not be,
Plague me with violent insistence.
No more, my eyes open and only the echo remains.

Sue Dunn

IN THE SHIT

      ... And the baby bear said
       '... And someone's been sleeping in my bed ... '

Oh I wish I could afford to be sleeping
But bi-weekly
I can't afford furniture . . . if I want to eat.
I can't get a loan . . . If I want to live long.
But short term I'll eat well, sleep well, sit well
Until . . .
PAYBACK!
Then . . .
CAN'T SIT!
CAN'T SLEEP!
CAN'T EAT!
I thought I was in the shit before . . .

      . . . And the baby bear said
      ' . . . And she's still in it!'

D-Zine

THE PHOTOGRAPH

Before you she stands, staring eyes,
    Eyes, deep pools of misery;
'Who dares photograph my suffering,
    You, white, dressed, well-fed.
    I have no bread.

    Let me die in peace,
    Let your picture-taking cease.
You have your buttered morning toast,
    Friends to talk to,
    Work to do.

All I have is bare ground,
    Empty of food,
    Empty of family,
    Empty of hope.
And I have no tomorrow.
    You just stare,
    You don't care.'

V S Petheram

NOT HAVE NOT HAVE-NOT

I speak from the other side of the street
Not have, not have-not, somewhere in between,
The one who, watching a busker scrutinise
Carriages for an audience who won't lower their eyes,
Scowl, mutter their disdain at his clothes
Or criticise, for his lack of permanent home,
Knows not whether to chance a straight smile,
To watch him play, or attempt to find
An advertisement I haven't read a million times
And rehearse again the sorry pantomime
Of avid interest in yet another soap-powder line
Fearing the accusation in his eyes
Of false concern, or intention to patronise
Believing me to be, in this our day and age,
An armchair Socialist whose memory fails
As the television images quickly fade,
Forgotten, and filed away under *another day*.
So, know you that with background noise
Of posters on the tube warning us away
From the pros who dupe us and enjoy
A standard of living, of dignity, devoid
There lies a quiet majority who look
Beyond the horizons of the tabloids,
Know not to believe all they read,
And do not merely stare, but attempt to see.

M Everingham

CIVIL WAR

The burning eye over the hill,
A source of life,
For those who kill,
For those who die -
A source of death.

In the wheat,
A soldier stands,
A heavy gun,
In sticky hands,
He aims to shoot,
He shoots to kill,
(The burning eye over the hill.)

In the street,
A woman stands,
A dying child,
In bloody hands,
She aims to stay,
Alive today.
(In fear and pain under the eye.)

And words of death,
Are on the breath,
Of those who lie,
Under the sun,
Under the sky,
Under the eye.

William Young

1994

In the modern world,
Nature has been replaced by technology,
Mysticism and magic by science,
Freedom by conformity,
Peace by war,
Beauty by destruction,
Liberty by confinement,
Friends by enemies,
Children by warriors,
What has become of the modern world?

Carolyne Pike (17)

UNTITLED

In they come
asking demanding
Out they go
in a world of their own
Don't they know?
Don't they care?
Is all that they want
a home of their own?
Do they cry?
Do they laugh?
Or do they simply work?
Don't they have dreams
of saving the world?
Or do they just want to
grow old,
having studied and worked
and done as they're told?

Sophie Pasarin

WHAT A PLACE!

Nelson Mandela House.
Ah, what a place to be born!
Evocative of sun, struggle
A promise of true freedom
Black and white together
All the world's chances
Wrapped up in a high rise tower.

The Vicarage
Ah, what a place to be born!
Evocative of sun, safety
Tea on the lawn for generations
Rich man, poor man together
Silver spoon chances from father
Wrapped up in his soul saving work.

How are such promises come to this?
Young blonde head on cold dark cheek
From opposite ends of the spectrum
Huddled for warmth in a doorway
Met in a sun-less city
Lost in a soul-less ecstasy.
Ah, what a place to die!

Jeffa Kay

BALANCE SHEET

In the cartels of the city bank
they don't think of the starving,
to be quite frank.
It never crosses the rubicon
of the financial mind
that poverty, like money,
is transmutable,
and guilt collective.
In the stick huts outside
the forgotten folly of Brasilia
the Indians are dying
swamped by the road systems
of progress.
The human factor
lies outside the neat whims
of the balance sheet.
Because it cannot be numbered
in currency
it cannot be counted.
In the cardboard caves
which pass for houses,
there are poor perishing.

Adrian Shaw

UNTITLED

Weathered by life.
Battered by circumstance.
This sand blasted stone
is all that remains
to remind;
of a once present crystal.

And in this cavity
within my breast
The place this stone
once did rest
Only a distant echo
have I left.

To serenade the tormented
screams of this child in time.

Jeremy Ryan

REPERCUSSIONS

Three months is quite enough
for the crude oil to permeate the graves
where there was time and inclination
and corpses intact enough to provide them.

We have reached the time
of the gaps and silences
the spaces which open up for the wounded
between desert and mountain.

For a time these regions
were thick with weaponry.
Now the only reports are of those suffering amidst suffering
ricocheting to the lofty nests of the crisis hawks.

The displaced attempt to populate
a landscape awe-inspiring yet featureless

where any fresh loaves of relief
are immediately stained with the icy mud
of a child's trampled face.

So it is quiet again
but for the vast shuffling of the lame congealing in their bid for safety
the creak of starched linen in the sad shake of a medic's head
the whisper of carrion as the flesh drops gently from the bone.

The interstices of repercussions we now inhabit
pondering pathetically whence came
such audacity
to pack these vacant landscapes with such certain armaments.

John Hamilton

BRIEF ENCOUNTER ON A LONDON TRANSPORT PLATFORM

You have grown old and wrinkled,
In youth colour was the problem,
Isolation then;

But now see me again,
Is my hair not grey like yours?
Are my wrinkles not proof

That we have traversed
Life's high and low ways?
That we have earned our place.

Old age is our great leveller,
Your skin has paled,
Mine has grown darker

From chillier and sunnier climes.

Why, are we not the same sisters
Under the skin?

Eileen Simpson

THE LAST CHILD

When the last child has gone
we will not see another day.
How can a world with so much
beauty in it, hurt so many
by cruelty or neglect.

In the brickfields of India,
and the brothels of the East,
they suffer for man's greed and
entertainment, are tortured and
butchered.

The death squads of Brazil leave
children's bodies in the gutter.
Teenagers sleep upon our streets,
and every night somewhere a child
muffles its cries of fear.

I do not wish to read another case,
or have my heart wrenched as another
horror is unfurled, but we should not
forget these obscenities - they are
real, they happen in our world.

D Leach

GOD'S BLUNDER

Human life?
        So weak . . . anaemic . . . rotten.
Words?
        So meaningless . . . less and less . . .
        Cosmic retribution circles the globe.

The iceman cometh . . .
        A heart freeze-up
        We grab what we think we need . . .
        never sure . . . never pure . . .

Whilst others . . . too weak to think or dream
        gasp and lisp their wants that never come.

False fecund wombs
        bring lives that fester
        on a mounting heap . . .
        whilst stomachs putrefy
        on rich dyspeptic living.

Whilst publicity prostitutes and media touts
        stimulate rank desires and greed
        depriving those in greater need.

Let's pull the weeds . . . lest the iceman cometh
        to tighten his grip until we freeze
        in abject fear . . . purged of hope.

Let's make *War on Want* . . . anew
        and love . . . in frozen hearts . . . renew.

Geoff Broady

DRESS

Wherever they look
They will see nothing.
Only things for sale.

And someone once said,
'Life is not a dress rehearsal,' and she thought,
They will see nothing ironing their costumes;
Thought is art.

She was so intent
on watching the show, laughing,
That she could not see
That she did not even
have a part.

Melanie Herring

TOYS OF WAR

There are no jobs and little reason for optimism,
so I spend my days doing voluntary work,
I don't get paid, I pass the time,
at a children's playgroup.
And I do as my father did with me,
I encourage the children when we play with wood,
to build, they make, swords, battleships and guns,
I help them to create, toys of war,
                toys of war.

The children are proud when together,
we've made something simple yet effective,
painted brightly, in the colours of their gang,
and I call myself a pacifist.
We take them to a children's playground,
the girls play nurses, the boys play soldiers,
I stand in no man's land, waiting for the outcome,
as they play on tanks and bombers,
                toys of war,
                toys of war.

We're living in a death culture,
an economy based on war,
Industries are geared towards the arms race,
we must dismantle it at the roots.
        And I do as my father did with me,
        I encourage the children when we play with wood,
        to build, they make swords, battleships and guns,
        I help them to create, toys of war,
                      toys of war,
                      toys of war.

Jon Perigud

INSIDE SADNESS

I cannot describe
the sadness deep inside.
From smug suburban fatness
the words come.

On a day of more than ordinary disorganisation
My children shout in righteous indignation
'No cake?'
and suddenly, I almost hate
my own children
for their fat gutted contentment
while a millennium of children
whisper
'No food?'
in desperation.
But, who can blame the children
in their ignorance.
They are only human.

Housewives complaining, whining,
Standing enfolded in plenty.
I have heard all the excuses.
'What can we do?
Nothing.
It is too big.
We might as well be happy.
We are only human.'

I hear what you say.
So what do I do?
Nothing.
It is too big
and I am only human.

But there is this sadness
deep inside.

P Jilks

UNTITLED

Did you see them last night?
Fragile limbs barely able to support swollen bodies.
Did you feel pity as you watched
skeletal fingers raised for today's handout?
Did you feel smug that your
coins had rattled the collecting tin?
Or did you, like me, feel only relief?
This is not my country, these are not my children, this is
                                                                not my problem.

Kathleen Wratten

CHOICE

I lay here,
In my nice safe bed,
Dreaming of you,
I know I will die fighting for you,
And be proud in that death,

Bombs explode all around you,
Killing your family and your friends,
You'll be tortured, starved,
And eventually murdered,
But tell me will you be proud to die?

It'll be my choice to die,
My choice to walk into your arms,
My choice to fight for your rights,
But it wasn't yours,
You can't escape; can't escape death,

I'll come soon,
To teach you,
To pray for you,
To die for you,
I'll come . . .

Gwenyth Webb

THE PENSIONER AND THE POT-PLANT

My life is haunted by the still
    suffering of pot-plants.
They and I are in it together till the end,
    which cannot be far off now.

We have looked through at the sun and yearned,
    hungered often in our hearts for . . . what?
For the wild? For some breath of glory and of liberation?

Now we ask ourselves, our leaves drooping, curling at the tips,
    is there, was there, anywhere such a thing as truth?
As true liberty? Our roots in darkness seeking
    find only the encircling pot. Our leaves,
Dumbly crying in moveless yearning, stretch
    gestures of pleading to the windowpanes
Where spatter the drops of dirty rain
    and beams of hooded sun
    veiled in the city's grime.

I hung above my fireplace once a tiger
    burning brighter than the gas, with savage eyes,
Teeth like white flames. But even he was framed,
    the illusion of his wildness didn't last.
I replaced him with a fatuous calendar of pups,
    and tried resignation and a colour TV set;
Saw moving pictures of wild mice at play
    and wild deer in their forests. So here we are,
    and was I, am I satisfied?

Ah, we have various ways of searching for our need.
It's not just I, the aspidistra and the tiger framed.
We are all trapped and snarling through the bars,
Trapped with our appetites, we stifle deep desires
    in sugar-coated follies.

Mary Cowan

THE RIGHT TO FEEL MY PAIN

People try to tell me pain is bad
They tell me the end is near
But all the problems I have had
Came through lack of pain
> I came into this world in pain
> Struggled against grappling hands
> My futile search for liberty
They gave me clothes and gave me shame
> To suffer was to be free
Now I understand their minds
> I give them my own key
To suffer pain I found
Has made me what is me
To go without my suffering
As much a part of me
As happiness or quiet thought
I could not be so free.

Dave Miller

MY FRIENDS, BIG CHANGES ARE ON THE WAY SOON

Consciousness must be raised, it seems to me
only too obvious. And poverty
terminated with extreme prejudice
in favour of the weak and weary souls.
Progress. Proof positive. We can take it!
Playing everywhere soon, here comes the new
millennium - and it's a second chance.

My heart soars with new-found optimism:
disease cured, hunger eradicated,
superior education for all,
weapons of doom now museums of life,
all chains pulverised into fashion jewels;
respect for the individual. Nuff said!

Spreading like news of a special free gift,
comes the future. Are you ready for this
new awareness and mental expansion?
Forget false prophets of the spectacle.
Global consciousness for the human race!
And what a considerable banquet -
feast of intellect, imagination;
sumptuous delicacy and love gift!

And listen up to me: No motive I
save my function as lucky messenger.
For I thought and felt around the corner,
tasted this freedom, gloried with the stars -
Hope in my heart, and memory of you.

Hazel Lezah

IN THESE DAYS

In these days of doing things
For companies not men
Does anyone remember
If there's an overall plan?

In these days of doing things
Like paying for our land
Does anybody wonder
Who owns these grains of sand?

It does seem an endless theme
Being me is just a dream
Sitting down is not for us
And being thus
Will be our loss.

In these days of doing things
And never counting cost
Will anyone ever stop
And make up for what we've lost?

Michael Wixon

TWO LIVES

She's twenty-nine,
working long hours to further
her high-flying career.
Her home is exquisitely tasteful,
her wardrobe packed with elegant clothes.
She drives a sleek scarlet sports car,
dines in expensive gourmet restaurants.
Choosing her career-moves carefully,
achieving her ambitions is easy.

He's just nine,
working long hours in
a damp, unwholesome, ill-lit factory.
He achieves too:
damaged eyesight, weakened lungs;
food to foil starvation;
the prospect of dying young:
he won't make twenty-nine.
He can't fight, can't beat the system.
Too young. Too weak.
No education. Zero power.
Non-existent choices,
no possible ambition:
except, perhaps,
simply to survive.

Fran Shortridge

UTOPIA?

A night's sleep,
A mouthful of fresh water,
A friendly smile,
The taste of something,
Freedom from pain,
A kind word,
Living till tomorrow,
Hope.

All Impossible.

A four poster bed,
A glass of champagne,
A comedy at the theatre,
 a Cordon Bleu meal,
Medical care,
Exhilarating company,
Living a lifetime,
An assured future.

All Possible.

What is Utopia?

When those for whom all is possible,
Provide what for others is impossible.

Suzanne Kushner

THERE IS A LESSON IN THAT

There is no free fruit,
fresh fruit. It depends
on the air it breathed.
What turns its skin
so suddenly into rot?
I fear Chernobyl or
some similar pollution.
The poor fruit just
grows as it should,
but what does it breathe?
You cannot test it
without a laboratory,
and you have to eat.
They eat poisoned fruit
all over this world.

Maureen Scott

HOMELESS

Like you,
my heart is homeless.

It sleeps out in the cold,
it begs for support.
I feed it titbits
to keep it alive.
It wanders around all day,
aimlessly.

But unlike you,
it lives in hope.

Peter Whiteley

A GULF BETWEEN

Mad man in the desert stuck his head into the sand
And felt his blood boil.
Heard the oil underground
And cried, 'This war cannot be won.'

Sad man in the desert plays his saxophone
Turns blue tears into rain
For his loss of faith in allegiances
And a war that can't be won.

Bad man in the desert building bunkers in the dunes
And fooling with the winds
That sift the landscape
With a button and a finger
On a pulse that can't be checked.

Dead man buried deep in situations
With a gulf between
The worlds he knew and feared
And hated when still living
In a world that can't be one.

Sad man in the desert soon will be at one
With the rich man and the poor man
The mad man and the bad man
In a war that can't be won.

David Hill

EARTH APPLES (FOR CHRISTOPHER COLUMBUS)

Of simple things, of seeds and soil,
Each reaps from their own gentle toil.
And underneath those lazy lanes,
Fecund nests for all labour's gains,
Lie incubating our new eggs,
Until harvest fills its vital sacks.
Such humane days, such harmless scenes,
Of simple things, of soil and seeds.

What reverie this? What wholesome theme?
Unseen the torment, unheard the screams.
Forgotten how from a far, fair isle
We first filled from *their* flowing soils.
How we got fat, how strong grew our bones,
how we weighed our stomachs with *their* earth stones.
Forgotten but with same imperious ways,
Exploited then as we exploit today.

Left only desert, furrows dry,
While in return we chop and fry
And force down dehydrated throats
Diets of death, desire and coke.
And then how proud we stand alone
And boast how what we reap we'd sown.
But no *taters* here, only thieved
Earth apples from our neighbour's trees.

Matthew Carter

WHY DO THEY SHOW ONLY THE WORST FACE OF OUR PEOPLE

Why do they show only the worst face of our people . . .
the hollow face of a suffering child,
who dies on the bed of a barren land
and whose marble eyes peer at the lens?
The young man fires his gun at the failure,
the failure to prevent the crumbling base
of a land where guns fill people's stomachs.
And here the camera film ends.

Why do they show only the worst face of our people . . .
when past the bones and behind the gun
there is a man shaking hands with his neighbour,
hands which have hardened from working all day?
A woman smiles as she feeds her son
with the milk from her herds which lines his ribs
and then leads the cattle to drink by the rocks
whilst singing with the branches with which the winds play.

Why do they show only the worst face of our people . . .
and drain the dignity which strengthens the weak
who are victims of power, weather, and war
and whose only water swells from their eyes?
Who knows best how best we can help?
Who decides which action to take?
Who gets the credit once smiles line their faces?
Listen to their voices as well as their cries!

Bethan Hatherall

BLUE SKY OVER BOSNIA

There was a blue sky over Bosnia
And once a bright sun shone.
But the sun sinks like lead
In a river of red,
For beneath, a war goes on.

Neighbour slaughters neighbour,
And friend kills former friend;
But no-one's sure
What they're fighting for,
Or when the violence will end.

Once there was warmth in Bosnia,
But now the sun has gone.
Thousands die
Under the blood-red sky,
And the madness carries on.

Emma Cable

THINK

Don't
Wanna
Have to
Think.
I shouldn't have to think
About you
You shouldn't even
Exist
Look around -
You're the only one of
Your kind
Around here
Go back to where you came from -
Your home
Go back home
If you've got a home
No home?
No problem -
Go to hell
Don't wanna have to think
About you.

Saeed Farouky

THE FLY

It is late, and on a windowsill
like a spark of electricity,
after seven short days of life,
I hear the death of a fly.

I weep more than others I have lost, still
I never did understand the futility
of people's lack of love for life.
I suppose some people deserve to die.

Andrew Nash

LATE NIGHT WATERSHED

It glistens deep, and spills and thrills,
And trickles down the cheek.
It takes its leave to run and weave,
As from the mouth it leaks.

From lips and skin, it trickles thin,
To a gutter shelter,
Mixing kin with raindrops in
The end that fate dealt her.

Now concealed, and far from pain,
Flooded to dilution,
Blood and the rains wash down the drains,
With violence, in solution.

Great swaying above, and
A disparate soul, dampened,
To ripples, a myriad,
So cold, still, calm -
Could one miss one
Among a million others?
One, by one, the lights go out.

James Mitchinson

RESPECT

Respect was taught with the smacking of a fist
Boots were raised to obtain obedience
And a gun was trained always at the forehead
Twitch finger clicking
Weights of iron were strung to eyes so to see and survive
would gouge eyesockets bursting
The nameless walked without name, crawled head hung downward
And language was denied by whips to the tongue, tongues nailed to the roadside
They dug their graves, they crawled inside, they prayed then died
Boulders into skulls crack, barbed wire hanging body rack
Rotting corpses, bubbling fat

Where have all the babies gone?

A mountain of clothes, a tower of shoes, mound of teeth, river of hair, valley of bone and ocean of blood.
In fire we burn, under oppression we are beaten
In famine we die.

V Greenfield

SHADOWS

Beautiful just like a holiday,
    facade of colour and beauty.
There in the shadows I put the uncared for,
    the unwanted.
I put them there so that you can ignore them,
    as in life.
So that if they're out of sight,
    they're out of mind.
But they're always there,
    peering from the shadows at you.
Why not try peering into the shadows.
    Sometime.

Robin Mason

WOMANKIND

Womankind, how long must you suffer
under the oppressive thumb of those
you say you love?

How much longer
will you continue to slave for oppressors
in full knowledge
in doing so, you're worsening the problem?

Because
womankind, as long as you slave for the oppressors
they'll expect you to.

Womankind
can't you see
you've built a rod for your own back?

Emma Jane Louise Buckley

WAR

War makes me think of death,
It makes me think of hate,
Families being ripped apart,
I wonder if it's worth it?

War makes me think of sadness,
It makes me think of tears,
Friends separated without farewell,
I wonder if it's worth it?

War makes me think of fear,
It makes me think of horror,
Brothers never seen again,
I know that it's not worth it.

David Leith (14)

LOVE

I filed a police report against you last night.
He asked me what my name was
and I thought of how subtly your accent comes
through when you pronounce my name.
He asked me for my address
and I thought of you feeding the cats
on the porch.
He asked me what colour hair you have
and I thought of all the hairs
you leave on the sink after you wash.
He asked me if you have any tattoos
and I recalled the tears you had in your eyes
when you spoke of your father.
He asked me how many times you hit me
and I remembered the pinkish glow of your face
as you arose from sleep in the morning.
He asked me how many times it happened before
and I thought of all your paintings
I have hanging throughout my house.
He asked me if I wanted to press charges.
I told him no
and turned my head
to hide the tears.

Andrea Warunek

M40

Neon jewels hang low in the sky
Adding man-made sparkle
Compounds crepuscular magic
An unlikely setting, necklace of twilight
Slung round grey, dirty asphalt along which,
In a heedless forgetting,
We speed towards night.

Jason Oddy

PARALLEL SEASONS

This spring
just before you stretched your limbs
into a topaz sky,
buds ready to be free,
the council came and lopped you,
to leave you
with a leper's hand.

Out on the baking street
she stretches her limbs
to anyone who'll look,
and points them to her baby,
hoping with wild eyes
for a better season.

Next spring
shoots will come forth
from those pitiful stubs,
it won't be quite like old times,
but there will
be blossoms.

By then perhaps
they will have found her
a way to earn a living
on the colony farm,
no time to beg now,
but some
for laughter.

Marian Griffin

DICTATORSHIP

Fear in faces
no-go places
truth suppressed
civil unrest

many lies
and sighs
and cries
as people die

hopes dissipate
lives stagnate
communities shatter
and the rich grow fatter.

Claire Barnes

BELOVED PEOPLE

These I know
and they shall
be nameless
he who is fined
for pushing *pot*
he who leads
an aimless life
she who busks
for a pittance
he who has
done GBH
and the one
whose nose
was broken
who in turn
wielded a
fryingpan
the transvestite
the lover of porn
the tramp
in and out of prison
all these I know
and love them all.

Joan R Gilmour

IMAGES

There is a sound on the wind
Of African babies dying.
Here, in the West, we are the damned
Because too few of us are crying.

The frozen image of a screaming mouth
Flickers impotently on the banker's harsh stare,
In another image, a child struggles for breath
But both lack the capital to make him aware.

For this is the *city,* where laughter bubbles above
A coffee-table collection of Third World agony.
As thousands, in black and white, bury the ones they love,
Obese money-merchants suck on cigars and sip at brandy.

Russell Mills

NAAMAN

Struggling for breath
in the oppressive grime of man,
I gazed into sullen London sky,
heavy with Joram's cloud.
From contemplation's core,
silent, soulful cries ebbed
formless words of emotion
onto the rock of reason.
O! Child of Naaman,
leper in heart and soul,
conquer foolish pride,
and cleanse your sores.
For unwisely reject hope,
and, unwashed by Jordan waters,
perish.

Jocelyn S Downey

DOESN'T MATTER

Somewhere, out there in the dark anonymity
of the cold, suburban streets . . .

A baby is crying
Someone is dying
A scream from the night
Death's razor-sharp bite
Someone's heart breaks
Another's soul aches
Feet pitter-patter
From the lives they have scattered
Doesn't matter

A woman's life violated
A young man is segregated
Age, colour, creed
Religious belief
No respect for the dead
Or the lives to be shed
Through the wars that rage on
From the dusk till the dawn
Lives lay in tatters
The spirit is shattered
Yet it still doesn't matter

Rainforests depleted
Secrets, secreted
Government deals
Informers that squeal
The lost and the homeless
Those who don't care less
Greed and hypocrisy
Hunger and poverty
The rich getting fatter
Off the poor on their platters
Who cares, does it matter?

Lindsey-Jane Stewart

PRISONER OF CONSCIENCE

The poet writes,
Each word a manifesto,
A freedom-fighter's gazette.
Her pen denies the muzzle.
The heart's blood is her ink,
Each blot a stain
No damask linen can launder.
The presses turn.
Their mellifluous print
Whispers sweet nothings
In the populace's ear.
Censored lies comb the air,
The stomach heaves beneath their surfeit.
In her cell
The poet sits,
A diamond scratching
On a windowpane.
The sun floods in
Through a noose of light.

Irena Uderska

NO-MAN'S LAND

This barren land drains
the blood from the dead
and the life from the living
only lost souls
can wander this mass-grave
searching for the life denied them
the sun cannot reach
this part of the earth
the sharp reek of decay
hangs in the air
as it would in the graveyard
of a dying world.

Fiona McCurdy (14)

NICARAGUAN RAINCOAT

'Here's one your size, red and blue.'
My fourteen-year-old nephew eyes it in disgust.
Then, remembering I'm the one who's coughing up the cash,
modifies his expression just enough to keep my generosity intact.
'I mean, it's alright, it's nice enough, Aunt C,
But it's not a Nevica, it's a Nevica I need.
They're altogether better, it's not just the name.
I got soaked last Friday wearing this old thing.'

Last Friday, I got soaked myself, walking to the meeting
to hear the speaker on Nicaragua tell us about her visit.
Young woman, drably dressed in shades of grey
(the kind of girl you'd say to, if she were yours,
why don't you wear some makeup, brighten up your clothes?)
'. . . And these are the coffee plants in bloom . . .'
clicking the remote control,
'And here, the coffee-pickers in the rain.
These long, black plastic sacks they wear,
the type we use for wrapping rubbish in,
are multipurpose over there. Everyone has one
to wear as raincoat in the storm,
then hang as curtain in a draughty room
or lay as *table* on the floor for tea. Isn't that incredible?
Just shows the difference in our lifestyles, don't you think?'

'What do you say, we adults have another drink?'
Birthday party over, he leaves. Sporting his new Nevica.
'That's a really super jacket, Carole. He's so pleased.
His old one might have done him for a bit, but you know
how fashion-conscious they are now. They all have one of those.
Still quite serviceable, though. I'll donate it to the Oxfam shop.
It'll serve some purpose, I suppose!'

Anne Murray

UNTITLED

The streetlight
hides
a multitude of
sins.
Leaning against the metal,
praying,
for money,
praying,
for her sins.
Pretending
joy,
and hiding
pain,
collecting her money,
praying,
once again.
The streetlight
hides
deaths
that cold night.

Catherine Barton

CHANGES

Don't look away
I was you yesterday.
Tomorrow who knows?
You may need this spare place
No conversation,
Huddled against the cold
Head aching
Pain, threatening to explode.
Determined to make it
Where?

NICARAGUAN RAINCOAT

'Here's one your size, red and blue.'
My fourteen-year-old nephew eyes it in disgust.
Then, remembering I'm the one who's coughing up the cash,
modifies his expression just enough to keep my generosity intact.
'I mean, it's alright, it's nice enough, Aunt C,
But it's not a Nevica, it's a Nevica I need.
They're altogether better, it's not just the name.
I got soaked last Friday wearing this old thing.'

Last Friday, I got soaked myself, walking to the meeting
to hear the speaker on Nicaragua tell us about her visit.
Young woman, drably dressed in shades of grey
(the kind of girl you'd say to, if she were yours,
why don't you wear some makeup, brighten up your clothes?)
'. . . And these are the coffee plants in bloom . . .'
clicking the remote control,
'And here, the coffee-pickers in the rain.
These long, black plastic sacks they wear,
the type we use for wrapping rubbish in,
are multipurpose over there. Everyone has one
to wear as raincoat in the storm,
then hang as curtain in a draughty room
or lay as *table* on the floor for tea. Isn't that incredible?
Just shows the difference in our lifestyles, don't you think?'

'What do you say, we adults have another drink?'
Birthday party over, he leaves. Sporting his new Nevica.
'That's a really super jacket, Carole. He's so pleased.
His old one might have done him for a bit, but you know
how fashion-conscious they are now. They all have one of those.
Still quite serviceable, though. I'll donate it to the Oxfam shop.
It'll serve some purpose, I suppose!'

Anne Murray

UNTITLED

The streetlight
hides
a multitude of
sins.
Leaning against the metal,
praying,
for money,
praying,
for her sins.
Pretending
joy,
and hiding
pain,
collecting her money,
praying,
once again.
The streetlight
hides
deaths
that cold night.

Catherine Barton

CHANGES

Don't look away
I was you yesterday.
Tomorrow who knows?
You may need this spare place
No conversation,
Huddled against the cold
Head aching
Pain, threatening to explode.
Determined to make it
Where?

Look at my hands
Dirt has no cares.
Remember the bath
Towels marked His and Hers.
Don't offer me money
Save it in reserve
Tomorrow you may remember me
The sad girl you saw yesterday.

Emma Shaw

THE SANDS

The sands roll on,
The children continue
To laugh,
Even when the food
Is gone,
And when they begin
To starve.
Now all the laughter's
Gone.
And aid arrives all
Too late.
Children remembered in a
Song,
Is this their only
Fate?
The politicians join
The fight.
But the battle's been and
Gone.
They promise money for
The plight.
And the sands roll on and on . . .

Nicholas Hayden

THE PRISON BOATS

An idea was floated in parliament
and among the Law Lords,
introducing the prison boat.

A fleet of three-yearers was the first,
leaving the harbour at dawn, hooting
to its future on the North Sea waves.

A warden-sailor told the BBC,
'We feel like guinea-pigs.'
One thief was in ecstasy:
'I grew up wanting to be a marine,
I can't believe my luck.'
And a woman who had been beaten
said she hoped for a freak wave, or else
a lost iceberg hovering just below the surface
like a white shark.

Soon ships were drifting from Cornwall to Scotland,
and this was a prison-free country.
One or two were mislaid; one, hijacked,
turned up in Argentina, tattered white flags waving.
(Several prisoners sued).

A politician praising the scheme
twenty years later said,
'We are nearly ready to rule the world again,'
then sat back and waited for the cheering.

Zoé Teale

THE TREE

Reaching to the sky
For all to see
The tree stood
Tall and majestic
Spreading its branches over the troubled earth.

The bark
Worn by time
Chipped by the harsh world of man
Displayed courage and hope for those who cared
But nobody did
Too involved in themselves to see what was happening.

Ignorant people
It is too late now
The tree has gone to your factories
To make a table
For your material needs.
Feel sorrow.

Rebecca Holyhead

THE LAST BUS CROWD

White artificial light
Comes to stop in the road
It's a cold and bitter day
Alright
For the last bus crowd

Some are tripping, some are stoned
Some just lie there drunk
Old men with the whisky-breath
(of hidden misery)
Stare in an unsure way at the number
While young men on social drugs
Count the growing crowd
Of ill,
Hungover,
And unsure humanity
That makes up the last bus crowd.

Jamie Spracklen

MESSAGE FROM THE MAYOR

'O yea! O yea! O yea!
Don't need stone statues anymore . . .
Got live-boxed-humans now
Sleepin' by the council house door,
Extolling
As plain as plain can be
Our new cut-price
Civic dignity . . .'

Reg Mares

OPERATION

There is an abscess
on the brain of the world
where surgeons of the negative
Gadaffi and Hussein
have speeches woven
into Middle-Eastern borders

Many are the doctors
and many operations
many are the races
and religious rites of man
one is the world
and the colour of our blood.

J G Paterson

START AGAIN

It wasn't really long ago
it wasn't really long
we tried to turn the world around
but it was still too strong
      (Start Again)

the graves of all the people
the hopes that lit them up
stretch across the century
always trip us up
>   *(Start Again)*

every time someone got up
to make a stand
out came lily-white hand
pointing at the past
>   *(Start Again)*

and the pursey-pink mouth
saying look across the wall
that's what these guys are after
they want to rule the world
>   *(Start Again)*

well all I've got to say now
it's time to start again
the blues have had their chance now
it's time to start again
>   *Start Again.*

Wolfgang Küchler

A TEENAGER'S DREAM

When I was five, a cowboy of course,
or maybe I'd join the local police force.
At seven it changed, I'd drive a big bus,
I'd take all the fares not making a fuss.
At fifteen, of course girls were the thing
all that I wanted was to buy her a ring.
At sixteen it's different, I live on the streets
I just long for a bed with crisp, clean sheets.

Paula Thomas

BURGER BAR (USA)

Going to buy a burger?
Perhaps you haven't heard
About the sorry saga
That leaves the jungle scarred.

Going to buy a burger?
Well, first the trees are burnt.
No, nothing for the logger,
A pasture's all they want.

Going to buy a burger?
The natives come off worst:
A finger on a trigger . . .
It's stupid to resist.

Going to buy a burger?
There sprouts a fragile turf,
But soil reserves are meagre:
The sward won't grow much beef.

Going to buy a burger?
You want an acre's worth?
Well, who's a greedy beggar . . .?
Five hundred's all you'll get.

Going to buy a burger?
Then onward pours the herd.
The clearing's lost its vigour:
The damage won't be hid.

Going to buy a burger?
You buy a native's curse;
You pay the forest's mugger;
Bring loss on all of us.

Going to buy a burger?

John Hatton Davidson

POETIC JUSTICE

What is there of me
in my surroundings
how do I fit in?
Take that old high-rise,
that new superstore
or that closed shipyard

I don't live there
I don't shop there
and I didn't work there.

So who does and who
built them, paid for them,
shaped them, closed them and why?

And what of me in all that?
I didn't pay, have a say.
hold a meeting, hold a banner
No - I didn't.
Is that what there is of me?

What about the news?
What is there of us
in the poverty, the wars, the laws?

We don't starve, we don't fight,
we don't vote for them.

So, in the menus of the world,
what taste do we have
of who goes hungry, goes war greedy,
or cooks up laws?

Indigestion? Injustice...
and who orders this, eats it,
suffers for it, is reflected
when we raise our glasses?so who does go hungry
go war greedy, or cook up laws?

Ruth Johannsen

THE LAMENT OF BRICK LANE

Evil impetuous,
Rampant, incestuous,
Ignorance nurtures her fast-growing son.
Escaping derision
With unnatural vision:
Sure Prejudice knows what his mother's begun.

So fast through the streets with a
Mind to kill Agape,
Bastard-child feeds off his mother and spouse.
How hard now the wind blows
With bricks through black windows
As Prejudice slaughters a child in each house.

Ralph J Lawrence Connor

RIGHTS

I have the right
To be fed,
Clothed and housed.
To be loved,
Given warmth;
To be proud.
Not to starve
On the streets
Empty and cold.
Despised and rejected
Or shunned
'Cause I'm old.
You tell me I'm useless,
A waste of your time.
You have your rights
So let me have mine.

Josephine Blyth

AMONG GIRLS IN WARTIME

Why do they pretend to enjoy
bread buttered so awkwardly,
Mummy?
They are not pretending, my dear.
So why are they turning their
slices upside-down,
Mummy?
Are they ashamed, or in fear,
Mummy?
Because of the war?
Mummy?

Krystyna Lejk

THE END OF THE CENTURY

It is born again
To the end of history
A piece of language
The wish of a new culture
The past in the present
Projecting the future

Utopia - the magic of ideas
Riding with rage
Over the apathy and inertness

New directions
Towards an unknown horizon:
The end of the century

Lores
That are born in thought
Are born again
In forms deformed.

Rodrigo Fino

HISTORY WILL TEACH US NOTHING

They deface
To leave the trace
Of the vicious face
Of their new race
Blind ignorance the base
Ideological mace.
Yet another case
Of that past place
Forgotten in haste
Its lessons we waste
Yesterday's dreams left to chase.
Shall we all savour the taste,
As we all fall from grace,
Slowly slide back into space,
Lights out human race.

Claire Motler

INJUSTICE IN GENERAL

Tatty juggler
    Soulful brilliance shining
        through rain!

'Move on,' - damn security
    guard.

Black - had it hard himself
    (in the fifties).

Such authority now,
    evicting South Bank's
        street artists.

Hypocrites! Genocide! Ignore!

Darin Brown

TV HEAVEN

Frozen, disparate voices drip
their hundredth, drip
their thousandth reply
as we sit cloaked in comfort
doing nothing,
watching idly as they die.

Distant, impoverished figures
move one moment,
become motionless the next
as we move untouched
in *TV Heaven*
never understanding why.

StephenThorne

ELEISON

The land is fertile.
The air is good.
There is abundant
wildlife. The
people torture, rape
and kill. Why?

Ralph Hoyte

SUGARWIRE

The AK74 assault rifle
Fires
650 rounds per minute.
It settles disputes at the speed of sound,
Now, can you leave home without one?

Paul Tremlett

UNTITLED

Who sets the standards?
The men wearing grey
Who can afford two lives
Take away your riches
And I'll reduce your choice

Vermin can breed at any level
Its a requirement is not restricted
      To visible dirt

You men in grey
Cast the first stone
She will bear it
In her innocence

Her only crime hunger
Her only vice herself
Men who set the standards
Will keep her in the gutter

She was born to expect nothing
But you lavish her with contempt
Close your eyes grey men
And you close your eyes to life

Your release
Is her prison
Your second life
Her condemnation

Take heed grey men
Fortunes change
One day the corpse
      Pulled from the river
May bear your name.

Amanda Watkins

UNTITLED

When suddenly you find
you don't know anything
anymore
and reaching on find
only the birds
for whom you scatter bread.

Steel Rosehip

UNFORGETTABLE

Grandpa remembers, the days of old.
The *good old days?* - 'No!'
Rapid fire, the rations few.
Nowhere safe, nowhere cosy,
Nowhere there is love!
Not the *good old days,* but the *bad old days,*
Forgotten by him not one!
An arm is lost, a friend is lost,
But memories still all remain!

Julie McDonald

WARMTH

Warmth to share,
Warmth to hold,
Warmth to hide yourself,
Warmth to get lost in,
Warmth to embrace,
Warmth to give,
Warmth to receive,
Warmth never to go cold,
Warmth for your hands to hold.

Christian Walker

UNTITLED

Green is the grass dancing on top of the earth.
Green is a leaf on the tree dancing bush to bush.
Green is a felt-tip pen colouring the top of a tree.
Green is a pencil colouring grass in a picture.
Green is tissue paper sticking it on to a collage.
Green is a feather on a beautiful peacock.
Green is an apple growing on a tree.
Green is paint, painting a lizard in the rainforest.

Annick Lauren McKenzie (8)

VICTIMS OF REALITY

Give me shelter
From the Arctic world
Whose only friend is you,
And only lover is me.

Save me from this desert highway, that we call life,
I can't stop your heartache
But I can stop the salt,
That takes away your love.

And when that cold bites in
Protect me with your innocence,
The only flower that's left
After the winter wakes.

And when that sun goes down
I'll stop your dreams from fading into the shadows.
And when your hope has gone
You can dream it back.

You saved me from the Arctic battle
That does not have a victor
Only victims of reality.
Whose dreams are shadows.

Binta Sultan

THREE CHILDREN

Last night in our lounge we sipped hot coffee
and saw, beyond the glow of our fire,
three starved, bone-poking babies,
their black forms sharply drawn,
frail, against the strength of white
stone steps. It was hard to tell
them boys or girls. Each movement was slow,
as though it was made in a foreign world.
Each turn of large heads
showed pain in huge eyes; their birdlike legs
too thin to carry the swollen bellies
ironically teated with pouting navels.
And, as they stood, like three separate
winter twigs, one was holding
his brother's hand; held it still
when he fell on the steps, his bones grinding
against the edge, protected by tissue -
paper-skin, white eyes dulled
with desperate pain beyond understanding.
The boy on his feet turned his face
in grief that had long-forgotten tears;
but still he held the womb's straw link,
held on while his brother, weak as a fairy-seed,
eased himself slowly to his feet.
Their image returned when I climbed the stairs,
pulling you up to our easy bed;
I let your hand slip as soon as I could;
freed my fingers to free my mind
from memories' thongs that bit and stung,
from an image of duty, of natural love,
a simple beauty that hurt too much
to hold in my head.

Cliff James

BEYOND THE STREETS

The pavements creak
Where hopes have perished
And abandoned gutters reek
Of mankind's misery and pain
Which lingers on
Between the well-heeled buildings
Where men make markets of their brains
And the voice of compassion is trapped
Interned beneath foundations
On which this whole damned dream is built
Brutal as a steely winter's dawn
That haunts the marrow of my bones
I hear the crashing silence torn
And the sickly dying sounds that moan
To God I do not trust my eyes
To see these streets where rotten lies
Retch in foul abandoned breath
To drop beyond this life this death.

Angus Landman

DISREGARDED

From expansive Savannah
To backstreets of Rome
Tempestuous lives
Surviving alone

Culture, tradition
Preserved to the last
To flourish regardless
Of hardship so vast
Physical attributes
History found
Superficially perfect
By pure vision we're bound

Life's romantic notions
Carry us through
The realisation
Of what's out of view

The underworld
The other side
Comprehended by dwellers
Of life's rough ride

To be born and to die
Unconditionally
In the substance between
Lies the diversity.

Kate Everington

THE WAY

Is that a light I see?
From the depths of my soul
I feel a black despair,
And long to find comfort
And peace.

Is that a light I see?
Showing me a better place
Where my burdened heart
Can find the answer
And rest.

Is that a light I see?
Raising me up so gently,
Soothing my aching breast,
Showing me the only way
To home.

Ann Wallis

MARCHING TO THE SAME TUNE

The blades are double-edged swords
dripping with fresh poppies
on an overgrown lawn:
concealing the tracks of those who
once promised an enlightened new dawn.

The blades are knee-deep in fodder
once more; benefits of technological progress
lie regressing on burnt-out sand,
shells on battlefield mires,
remnants rusting in no-man's land.

We do not kill our enemies:
they simply kill each other.

Sean McMahon

FIEND

'You,' Cockney skinheads shout,
'Are just a foreign fiend.
'By you, we are demeaned!'
Each is a proud, white lout

Who pushes me about.
On blood, they must be weaned.
Against me, they have leaned.
'You should soon be thrown out,'

They bawl, 'since you are brown.
'We're white, and so we're great.'
Their London is a town
Where everything is hate
Like acid bound to drown
Love in a crumbling state . . .

Zehria Ibrahimi

CHRISTMAS - BLACK AND WHITE - 1993

The house was filled with cooking smells
The Christmas tree bedecked with baubles
And bright tinsel and tiny candles.
The floor was strewn untidily
With shiny wrapping paper discarded in haste
To get at the presents within.
The laughter of children could be heard
As they put on their *Sunday best*
Ready to go to church.
They would sing carols
And kneel by the Nativity
Heads bent in awe!

In Somalia an infant squats on the ground
Large eyes gazing sightless
No clothing to protect him from the searing temperatures
His matchstick arms and swollen belly
Speak silently of his lack of food.
He does not have the energy to complain
He has no mother to protect him
He belongs to nowhere and to no-one.
He has no name, no past,
And will have no future
Till death claims him and his tiny body
Will be hastily thrown into a hole
With others like himself
For whom no-one cares.

May we who have too much
Never forget those
Who have too little.

Jane Nyman

THE WAY TO STOP

The way to stop bullets
Is in your teeth
The way to stop autocracy
Is with bullets
Bullets have teeth.

Autocracy has pleats and pages
and bullet hole
and teeth marks

The way to stop pleated autocracy
Is with bullets in your teeth
Another word for bullets in your teeth
Is
Words.

Ruth Faulkner

SEARCH FOR CREDENCE AND SANCTUARY

Curiosity beckons
He walks the path, lethargically
Visions, glimpses of life, adorn his mind
in his midst, the gates.
Wrought with age, timeless beauty
A wonder filling every inch of vision
turning back . . .
Not entering.
Suffer not the pain . . . the anguish,
Great burden of life
Feel not the weight of the penance chain
shake free
Take knowledge from the battle
not suffering until the end.

Awake my golden child.

Gordon Gellatly

WAR 1 - 2 - ?

Take one dictionary
cut into many, many pieces
as many pieces as words.
Strew them to the wind at
the cliff of dreams and it's
all only words -
Have they stopped counting yet
when is a war, not a war,
when is want satiated
God has a sense of humour
of sorts
It all depends on the reader
really
War, what is it good for?
Profit, mainly, I don't read
Newspapers much these days
looking back, they say the
same thing over and over
again.
All the news fits all the pages
and all the want throughout
all ages, mount up and
multiply, mount up and
mystify. Young men think
they are invulnerable, will
make a difference
old men reorganise and
try plan b, plan c
on and on
over and out.

Adam Kisch

A LITTLE RYE

Help! Help us live or help us die,
Here we lie, with no more ties.
The village of my childhood
Is no more my neighbourhood,
I have lost my selfhood,
My body is wood.

My head aches, my heart has a stake,
My stomach is a snake.

Help! Help us live or help us die,
All for a little rye!

John Conolly

THE HOMELESS

Some take refuge in silence,
huddling fetally,
having no home but that one remembrance.

Some speak uncontainably,
having no walls to hold the words in.

Some rage at each other,
having no space to save rage for those
who are anyhow too sheltered
from their own hearts to care.

Chris Mandell

BLESSED ARE THE MERCIFUL

He who, in the race for life,
Pursuit of greed and gain,
Looks neither to the left not right
      the weaker to sustain.

Does not, in conscience, run at ease
Guilt-blistered to the soul,
His panting breath, the hollow sweat
      make not attainment whole.

Somewhere along the naked route
The naked victims wailed
Bereft of all, souls hanging out.
      To heed - to victor failed

While tripping over casualties
To snatch the prize afar -
Compassion lost on faculties
      as love and mercy are.

His Midas Touch turns not to gold
As ghosts come home to roost,
Awake , asleep, the doors unfold
      his consciences to boost.

The widow sheds her flow of tears,
The glut has none to spare;
His arid soul belies dark fears
      On judgement day - BEWARE.

Stella Gilder

PICTURES FROM AFRICA

Strange fruit, born of the desert dust
These beetle babes
Big bellied, legs like sticks.
Around blank eyes a crust
Where insects crawl,
Too weak to cry, they prick
Our guilty hearts to rage,
  . . . until we turn the page.

Jaquetta Benjamin

ETHNIC MINORITY

What is this 'ethnic minority' business?
Him say: What is your ethnic origin
- British
- US citizen
- Ethnic minority, or others?

Can't they even use their name
Them all as important as you, you know
They ain't no minority in their own land
So why should they be ethnic here?
Our government like to put everyone in boxes
And stack them up in blocks.

Kirsten Pollard

LIFE LINE

A tiny baby cries
his mother seeks for food
smothered by the heat.

Gathering grains of wheat
the boy fights for his find
from the desperate crowd.

The boy half asleep
bare legs fighting the wilting vines
where the water lies.

The relentless sun
dries up the village's crop
their harvest incomplete.

Like dust swirling
through the dried up land
at the news of his death.

Jennifer Tucket

WORK HARD

Stressed out
burn-outs
twitching their way
through
another day
trying to find
the reasons
they used
to live
by
making silent
excuses for
ambitions
unrealised
looking for
weakness in others
because
they have
no
strength in
themselves
ignoring confrontations
taking too many
sick
days
off
saving up
their lives
for their
two week
holiday.

Steve Verrall

THE DAGGER

The dagger may turn to the left or to the right,
But each time it murders and mains
Just a few more.
Each side claiming truth over the other,
Both professing to have the answers
But neither possessing any,
Inflicting the opinions, they hold
us, with them.
Ever damning consequences to their victims.
We, merely the fox in the hunt.
Chasing, capturing, savaging,
Mutilating, the truth.
Blackmailing us, with empty promises,
To put a mark against their name,
Take sides, face the enemy.
Once succeeded, forgotten,
Is their side of the bargain,
Free to rule without question,
But for quintennial restraints on their tryranny.
Their freedom is our prison,
Yet fortunate we are, to live under demoncracy.

Paul Sharkey

OUR THIRD WORLD

Daily, we calmly live with injustice,
Ignoring essential signs of decay;
Foresight and vision our leaders dismiss.

Blind eyes toward internal politics,
Forgetting the role our country can play;
Daily, we calmly live with injustice.

Colonists went and stripped with avarice,
Creating the problems we have today;
Foresight and vision our leaders dismiss.

Famine and refugees fuel prejudice,
Death and disease are the rules they obey.
Daily we calmly live with injustice,

Vaccines and pills are our answers to this
But we will not give our answers away;
Foresight and vision our leaders dismiss,

Tell us it's wrong that ignorance is bliss,
Let's wipe out the causes without delay.
Daily, we calmly live with injustice -
Foresight and vision our leaders dismiss.

Patricia Hynes

GOODBYE CENTURY

There was a fire
That ran around
Between the walls
And dreams snapped
Like wishbones
Under their own
Sallow load

But I didn't
Make a phone ring
In a fire station
For I am
No innocent

I too collaborated
With the flames
And watched
The world shrink
Until myself alone
Balanced on
A cinder ball.

Gemma Reynolds

ON FEELING A COMING OF A CHILL

all round the world rich people grabbing up poor peoples' heat
let me tell you 'bout a few places where
rich peoples grabbing up poor peoples' right to heat

in England in an increasing cold/we are told -
(with the straightest of a face - damn government don't even feel no
disgrace) - that they'll tax the fuel in our homes
so (I conclude) when we get cold **we should just be bold**/and face
it or put on yet another jumper/can't-turn-up-the-heat-cause
all over the world rich peoples grabbing up/poor peoples' right to
heat.
then on being a Kurdish refugee amidst the war/ain't got a clue
                                                     what's in store
for you/when you hit that Turkish border/you'd think that the
                                          government might **offer**
to give you some real cover/help keep out the frost/and battle
                                                      the snow
cause you been runnin'/got nowhere else to go/and you're
                         living on wintertime-mountainside edge
on top of lack of food and fuel/ever'one disclaiming responsibility
                                                        for you
as you try to keep your family warm but your children die of
                                    cold and hunger before the dawn
what can be said? some of it is
one more case of rich peoples denying poor peoples' right to heat

where can you escape?/don't even think 'bout go living in the states
can't even afford to keep out the cold - or so I'm told
see I heard it read in the Guardian today/that Clinton thinks that
$12.50 could pay/ for his second-hand long johns when he
                                                       threw them out
it's a fact I doubt/ but still/I wanna **SHOUT** when I hear 'Mr Fierce'
                                             propose/that only $8
dispos-able
cash a month/on top of stamps for food/may be the rule
for some on welfare/do you think he cares?

Nooo- when-it-comes-to-the-crunch-and-some-feel-a-chill
seems-they-don't-maintain-that-right-to-keep-warm-still
cause can't even afford to buy - not new/not secondhand-one damn
pair of winter long johns.
See now how in far too many places/in a great too many places/rich
people/rich people/rich people grabbing up licking up- soaking
up/poor peoples right to heat.

Andry Anastasiou

QUESTION

Ignore your cupboards,
shopping trolleys and handbags;
they are empty.
Play blind to sickly, blinking faces,
that peer from gloomy, hidden places.
Deaf to city streets whimpering
and the cold, cruel whistling
of desperate souls.
Just fill in this here questionnaire,
and on a scale of one to ten,
just how far can we push you, eh?

Gareth Cavill

WORDS

Stop rattling your sabre in its scabbard
Impotent in your rage.
Hands crushed by crippled bones
have already sprawled across some dirty page
blood stained words of defiance.

Halfway across the world
Upon some half lit stage
Another mouth stands agape
To repeat the words they heard
from one who saw.

D Kennedy

MY FAVOURITE WAR

The thoughts way down my head weigh down my head
So I walk looking at the floor
Thinking that they've got it wrong
Wondering who could get it right . . .

Let's have a war worse than before
They've all been fought for unites
So let's fight for divides -
A war with six billion sides
They're not you, kill 'em.

My favourite war never seen before,
One to make the earth move
One against one against one
Until we're all gone
But for the one who won,

Lift up your head we are alone.
Lift up your head we are our own.
There is no world but a world of worlds
Pure evil is speaking for many.
Difference should unite-
I might have got this wrong-
We have got to get it right.

Lift up your head
The world is just a crystal glass
The wrong people are singing
Architecture has no future
Go through your address book and pray
Because a song is not enough to take away
A question mark
And give peace a full stop

Mostafa Woola

THE YELLOW SKY

That morning when the potato tops rusted,
the mangle rested and the well ran dry
and the turf house leaned like a pumpkin
against the yellow sky.

there was a fire lit in the turf house
and a thin noise of crying,
and under the skinny sheets a woman
wadded with cloth against bleeding.

That morning her man went to the fields
after a shy pause at the end of her bed,
trying not to pick out the smell of her blood,
but she turned and was quiet.

All day the yellow sky walked on the turves
and she thought of things heavy to handle,
her dreams sweated with burdens,
the bump and grind of her mangle.

All day the child creaked in her cradle
like a fire as it sinks
and the woman crooned when she was able
across the impossible inches.

At that moment at the horizon there came a horseman
pressed to the saddle, galloping, galloping
fast as the whoop of an ambulance siren -
and just as unlikely. What happened
was slower and all of a piece.
She died. He lived (the man in the fields),
the child got by on a crust
and lived to be thirty, with sons. In the end
we came to be born too. Just.

Helen Dunmore

BARD AT THE BAR! (WE GET REQUESTS)

Why don't you write poems about . . .
. . . Urban deprivations?
Or trains that hardly run to time,
at British Railway stations!

The breakdown of social fabric -
- TV programmes - marriages!
The continuing refinement of . . .
'infernal combustion carriages'.

Government, white paper policies,
relating to this and that.
Various wars the sports result scores;
And the fact that the worlds not flat!

Those traffic jams on motorways,
and all the rising crime.
Bet you could think of lots to say!
Then write it down in rhyme!
A verse about our factory, us workers
who clock in.
Our wages and conditions, the decibels
of DIN!

And what of all the starving folk,
an all those unemployed?
Why don't you write on things like
that? It makes me so annoyed!

The rising tax, on beer and fags,
the fluctuating pound!
Oh Yeah! and that reminds me?
I believe it's your next round!

Paul Nicklin

ONE QUESTION FROM A BULLET

I want to give being a bullet
I've been a bullet too long

I want to be an innocent coin
in the hand of a child
and be squeezed through the slot
of a bubblegum machine

I want to give up being a bullet
I've been a bullet too long

I want to be a good luck seed
lying idle in somebody's pocket
or some ordinary little stone
on the way to becoming an earring
or just lying there unknown
among a crowd of other ordinary stones

I want to give up being a bullet
I've been a bullet too long

The question is
Can you give up being a killer?

John Agard

THE HERO AT THE END OF THE CENTURY

through the window I could see her
get on her knees, she had no other
choice.

I had noticed a flurry of colour
in the window across and to the
side, just below.

Found my binoculars.

A struggling shape arms and legs
three or four men arms flailing
one or two fists the threat of more.

Surrounded. Quite still. Light
reflecting. A glare - a closer look -
a large knife.

Obvious persuasion,

through the window, I could see her
get on her knees, she had no other
choice.

Eamonn O'Neill

THE THIRD SIDE

We hated them,
They hated us.
We fought them,
They fought us.
We killed them,
They killed us.
We lost family and home,
They lost family and home.
We are alone,
They are alone.
Together the same.
Victims.

Lea Farmer

SARAJEVO

A photograph, subtle as a jackboot,
Screams at the reader.
Yet, it is not the number of children,
Lost in the fading depth of field,
That stops the turning page
But
One face.
Her eyes, cod blank,
Crouch behind bars of lashes.
Her teeth are clamped fast
Holding in the vacuum that is the child.

Next to the lolling mouths
And saliva webs of her siblings
She rebukes my cathartic charity
And waits, stubble-headed and shadow engraved,
denying me
As I, in turning the page, deny her.

Christopher Straker

DEATH

i was born
and stood before the
tree of visions mesmerised,
while death stole up behind
and tapped me softly
on the
neck and
turning in
surprise, the
light of life went

Jamie Muir

DROPPING PENNIES

I see
the self-righteous people
In their
M
I
S
E
R
L
Y

T
O
W
E
R
S

Dropping pennies down for the slaves
H   U   T   F
O   P   H   O
L   E   U
D   N
I   D
N   A
G   T
                            I
                            O
                            N
                            S

Hammy

CARDBOARD AVENUE

Yesterday . . .
it was cold outside
Rays of dawn streaked pale-blue skies
The cloak of night was pulled away
and I live again another day

Today . . .
North winds bring hints of winter
Scourge of the old and poor
Some can trap the heat inside
but I cannot close my door

My door is always open
but people close their door on me
whatever happened to *us* and *we*
in this place called society?

Who cares if I bathe a hundred times
as rain pours continuously
into my sittingroom, the scene of crimes
on the roadside and the street corner

I want not pity nor disdain
I seek not the golden fleece
but shelter for my frozen limbs
might warm me and bring lasting peace

And then if I should drift away
like a wisp of smoke on a cloudy day
into the nothingness of oblivion
maybe I'll again be free
of this thing called society.

Olawale Akinlade

THE DAY BEFORE

The war began the day before and will last beyond tomorrow.
All too quickly we ignore the heartache, pain and sorrow.

People starve and friends now fight, forced onto a different side
No longer can they know what's right - to whom do they confide?
A different force controls their lives, living from day to day.
A losing battle to survive. And why? No-one can say.
The answer lies beyond their reach, is it really in our hands?
Who are we to dictate or preach? Dividing up their lands.

The war began the day before and will never end tomorrow.
It's important we do not ignore the pain, the death, the sorrow.

Julia Black

IN THE COLD

I sit here in the cold
and I wonder.

Rough on the streets,
only a box to sleep under.
Male, female, young or old
the streets don't discriminate
they take numbers untold.
Is this their life, is this their fate?

I sit here in the cold
and I wonder.

Milly Rumba

THE GREEDY WEST

My pain is so intense
I would destroy the whole world
to eliminate it,
'It's naive to think of world disarmament.'

I am starved
I could devour the whole world
and not be satisfied,
'We can't afford to spend more of our GNP on aid.'

My rage is so immense
I sit inert
consumed by it,
'I simply haven't the energy to do more.'

How can I relinquish
my comforts and defences
when I am so deprived?
'I don't think you appreciate how much I already give.'

I have been so hurt
that I am entitled to everything
in compensation,
'I can't meet all the demands made on me as it is.'

The more you guilt-trip me
with film of dying children
the more I cling to what I have,
'I sometimes feel we're just being manipulated.'

How can I not hate
the ugly, starving, injured child
who makes me see myself?
'Is it any wonder we're suffering from compassion-fatigue?'

Anne Wade

ONE NIGHT'S VICTORY

The sweat starts to pour
As he opens my door
In the pillow I hide my shame

He kneels by my bed
Starts stroking my head
And softly he calls my name

I begin to cry
When he tells me that lie
'I'm not going to hurt you again.'

I beg of him 'no'
I want him to go
I don't want to suffer more pain

He walks to the door
Then calls me once more
To wish me a pleasant sleep

Once more I have won
He's left me alone
Alone to just silently weep.

Dirkwood Marley Wad